ChAMbers
of
Consciousness
Assemblage Points for
Self-Governed Planetary Community

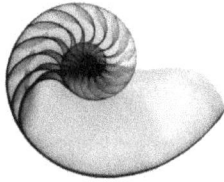

By Leah LaChapelle
©2018

ISBN: 978-0-9827906-6-3
Out There Books Publishing
OutThereBooks.com
Cover by Cheryl-Rae.com

DEDICATION

It is to each and everyone in the SCircle of Intention,
who compose my own life-giving and 5D group
cherished ChAMber of Consciousness in Austin, Texas,
that I express my gratitude and appreciation for
authentic community.
In this esteemed scircle, I can safely REVEAL mySelf
in ongoing Self-discovery,
as a vital, Soul-aware presence in galactic service on Earth.
Thank you for faithfully
holding the current with me, and for Our beloved planet.

There is only One scircle.

FOR THE READER…..

ChAMbers of Consciousness are where We become
5th dimensional New Paradigmers together,
and where you will only be joyously responsible for you.
It will take learning and practicing how to create with All others,
in a new vibrational frequency.
For those of Us who would like to be a part of assembling a
paradigm of lasting planetary peace and Freedom,
ChAMbers of Consciousness is offered as
a guidebook for any 5D group.

Contents

FOREWARD

Conscious ChAMbering:
Crossing the Threshold into the Fifth Dimension (5D)

Everyone loves a secret passage door…..especially the mysterious kind that has been shrouded in vines, blended into the foliage, deep within a cathedral forest, having been long forgotten. And then by a twist of fate, a worthy journeyman newly discovers it once more. Just happening to have the gnosis, heart, and Soul that matches the unique frequency code, the door magically opens to the journeyman's noble intention, and leads him out of the familiar, and into an altogether new and shining future.

This sounds like a fairy tale, but there is a mystical door, deep within the dense forest of Our perceived reality. It is this threshold which is the entry point to peace on Earth, abundance, healthy cooperation, and Freedom for Humanity. This passage to peace that leads out of the illusory and treacherously controlled, dualistic matrix, has simply been blocked by the brambles of the dark and untransformed lower dimensions.

Although occluded, this healing passageway, has always been there, throughout the Ages. All who have chosen to venture over this threshold have found themSelves transformed. Until now, only the very few have so much as encountered this passageway. There are even fewer who have actually made it across the threshold—and back again—to describe the experience to expectant others, as accessible, desirable, natural, and *doable*.

In terms of the majority, the existence of this mystical door has been deemed unscientific, irrelevant, a fantasy, non-existent, or simply unattainable. It has remained shrouded to all 3rd dimensional attempts to find it. To those who do at least encounter it and attempt to open it by means of their painstaking 3D efforts, it remains immovable and steadfastly shut. Regardless of the righteous efforting put forth, including violent force, this seemingly intractable door has stubbornly barred the way that leads to lasting Peace for Earth inhabitants.

One might ask, why not just use the key? A tangible key would be of no use - for this unconventional door has no key hole, but responds only to frequency. And so for most, the door has remained impenetrable, shrouded in mythology, and thus relegated to esotericism and arcane mystery schools. It has remained locked, until now that is, that the right strength of convergent energetic frequency has arrived!

~ ~ ~ ~ ~

5D is the non-polarization of 3D, which is necessary to Human continuance, by merging Science, Philosophy, and Spirituality, and leading with the heart.
"ChAMbering" is a relational invitation into 5D, inspired by and emphasizing, the frequency of "I AM" of Presence.

~ ~ ~ ~ ~

This non-fiction book, *ChAMbers of Consciousness,* is a companion guidebook to my fictional novel *Soul Shade*, and is written for those galactic explorers who choose to know more about effectively flowing in group-Soul 5D consciousness dynamics. It is a reference tool for would-be peaceful planetary "secret door openers", "threshold crossers" ….. and "cosmic streakers", such as the 5D-impassioned *Soul Shade* main characters.

Who exactly are these "pathfinders" who are fascinated with

this secret door passageway?
They are Human beings.....
.....WHO HAVE AT LEAST ONE THING IN COMMON.

They may not have the same cultural, ethnic, social, economic, educational, or religious backgrounds, nor agree politically, intellectually, philosophically, or on personal morality. It may be surprising, but that one thing is not their knowledge of sacred texts or science, or physics, or their socially concerned activism, or that their 3rd eye is open.   These curious beings won't have all the answers, but there is one thing they all share.

They have a "knowing" that there is something really "off", or unhealthy, or inherently just flat wrong about Our reality and what governs it. They know and feel that as "scentient" beings, Our natural state is to be Free, and that Humanity has been denied that Freedom, having been offered deception and lies and enslavement in its stead.   They know that scarcity is an imprisoning false matrix.   They know that both historically and currently, this 3D dualistic fear-based reality is an imposed, controlled, hierarchically-driven .....illusion.

They may not know exactly how it may be possible to
liberate Humanity from this condition,
BUT,,,,,THEY KNOW THEY MUST AT LEAST TRY.

Participation in a chAMber of consciousness as outlined in this little book, will REVEAL the whereabouts of the secret door, and the frequency code that opens it.   From the heart of a chAMber, a vibration emanates in a spiraling energy. As a microcosm of new Soul-aware Humanity, it provides the global positioning that takes Us deep into the forest of the two-fold knowing that:
1.) Judgemental negative emotion cannot cross the threshold;
2.) We're ALL crossing the threshold together, as One.

~ ~ ~ ~ ~

Living is
To remember,
when faced with something so simple
That only a child could do it
To speak the truth that I once spoke
To know love as I once knew it
To know that here is the plan, and now is the dream
To seek the light, and turn to it.
The key to the door is opening it,
The door is going through it.

Poem by Catherine Wiedmann;
Facebook: Catherine Wiedmann

~ ~ ~ ~ ~

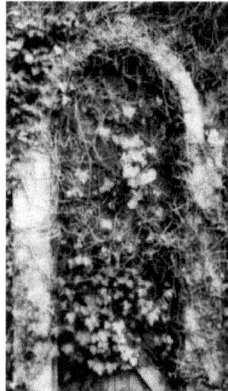

INTRODUCING

ChAMbers of Consciousness
(Cs of C)

Consciousness chAMbers are comprised of Human beings who are alive in the wakefulness of the ineffable "I AM" Presence. This kind of 5th dimensional chAMber signifies the supernal "AM" within "chAMber", with AM in upper case. (For the more agnostic reader, think in terms of impersonal existence.)

When Human beings purposefully coalesce to form a chAMber of consciousness, their inner personal transformational work has the opportunity to be catalyzed within a microcosm of Earth inhabitants. The refining energy of a C of C calls forth a new capacity, for each participant to emerge from the limitations of the 3rd dimension of consciousness (3D), as a new 5th dimensionally conscious Human archetype. Think caterpillar, chrysalis and butterfly, only in terms of Humans! This book is a support manual for group application for experiencing Our Human metamorphosis/evolution from 3D (extreme polarization in duality) through 4D (opening of the heart) to 5D (non-hierarchical, non-polarized Oneness.)

~ ~ ~ ~ ~

Generally speaking, BASIC CHAMBERS are absolutely everywhere in natural Life….. The word "chamber" is integral in Music, Law, Physics, Politics, Medicine, Science, Science Fiction, Mathematics, Engineering, Theology and every categorization of "–ology". Let's take a look at what a chamber is, by definition, which is what led me to the idea of the "chAMber-ing" of consciousness.

*A generic *"chamber"* is a dedicated space, the interior of which allows for a very particular purpose, action, or empowerment to be housed or catalyzed.

*A *"chamber"* is a private room, cavity, or compartment, and is innately interiorized in its essence.

There is one thing that all types of "chambers" have in common, whether existing as an ancient artifact, in current day, or futuristically. They are distinguished by what happens on the <u>INSIDE</u> of them.

Look below at all of the many examples of various chambers found in the English language.

In the Great Pyramid of Giza:

Queen's ___ *Chamber*
King's ___ *Chamber*
Upper ___ *Chamber*
Inner ___ *Chamber*
Initiation ___ *Chamber*
Subterranean ___ *Chamber*
Main ___ *Chamber*
Burial ___ *Chamber*
Chamber ___ of Reflection

Common Chambers:

chamber ___ of commerce
*chambers*___ of the eye, ear, and brain
*chambers*___ of a gun
*chambers*___ of the Human heart (4)
chamber ___ of horrors
chamber ___ music
chamber ___ orchestra
chamber ___ cradle to support an object

chamber ___ another word for bedroom
Bridal ___ *chamber*
Debate ___ *chamber*
Holy ___ *chamber*
Innermost/inner court ___ *chamber* (Bible)
Judge's ___ *chambers*
Legislative ___ *chambers*
Secret ___ *chamber*
Torture ___ *chamber*

The more one investigates usages for the word "chamber", the deeper into science AND science "fiction" you go.

In Science: (inexhaustive)

Accelerator___*chamber*
Activation/Deactivation ___*chamber*
Aerosol___*chamber*
Air___*chamber*
Biology Choice___*chamber*
Bubble___*chamber*
Burn___*chamber*
Cloaking___*chamber*
Cloud___*chamber*
Combustion___*chamber*
Compression___*chamber*
Cryogenic___*chamber*
Decloaking___*chamber*
Decompression___*chamber*
Deprivation___*chamber*
Diffusion___*chamber*
Drift___*chamber*
Echo___*chamber*

Fluid___ *chamber*
Fruiting___*chamber*
Gas___*chamber*
Growth___ *chamber*
Hologram___ *chamber*
Hyperbaric Oxygen___*chamber*
Imaging___*chamber*
Incubation___ *chamber*
Induction___ *chamber*
Initiation___*chamber*
Isolation___*chamber*
Leaf___*chamber*
Magma___*chamber*
Nautilus___*chamber*
Photographic___*chamber*
Plenum___*chamber*
Pollen___*chamber*
Pressure___*chamber*
Quantum___*chamber*
Recompression___*chamber*
Spark___*chamber*
Storm___*chamber*
Test___*chamber*
Transfer___*chamber*
Vacuum___*chamber*
ETC.

And in Science *"Fiction"*:

A.I.___ *chamber*
Anti-gravity___ *chamber*
Cryo Containment___ *chamber*

Disintegration___ *chamber*
Etheric Sleep ___ *chamber*
Healing___ *chamber*
Hibernation___ *chamber*
Hyperbolic Time ___ *chamber*
Infinity___ *chamber*
Integration___ *chamber*
Light Synthesis___ *chamber*
Materialization___ *chamber*
Oracle___*chamber*
Portal ___ *chamber*
Quantum Transfiguration *chamber*___ of Light
Saturation___ *chamber*
Stasis___ *chamber*
Suspension___ *chamber*
Tachyon___ *chamber*
Teleportation ___ *chamber*
ETC.

AND NOW,,,,, cropping up on Our planet at the end of this Age, are groups of awake, aware, alive people who are assisting in proactive, Self-empowering, world-transforming, interdependent assembly into energetic points that are registering as planetary community within a New Paradigm. These groups could be called many things. I call them: *ChAMbers* ___of Consciousness. You could definitely say that whatever is being accomplished in a ChAMber of Consciousness, is "an *inside* job"! These evolutionary chAMbers are proof positive that Humans are evolving beyond the Old Paradigm dualistic version of life, into a possibility for whole and peaceful, Self-determined community on a planetary level.

The content of this how-to book, has been learned through years of experimenting within group energy, by regularly participating in and facilitating 3D-to-4D-to-5D group experientials. *ChAMbers of*

Consciousness is written for anyone on their path, of any personality type, spanning the generations, with any skill set, any culture and background, who is reaching for more ability to bring forth balance and Freedom for themSelves and for Our world *in every Life situation.* The focus is on Self-empowerment, transformational discernment and manifestation, and a transcendent grace of being. It is my hope that *ChAMbers of Consciousness* will assist the reader in attracting fellow Humans with whom to process and evolve naturally, through the opening of the heart. Recalibrating the vibrational frequency of Our species for a New 5D Paradigm is the conscious chAMbering experience. It is joy itself, that beckons Us to new levels of observing OurSelves as planetary influencers and liberators, and stretching as the eternal Souls that We are.

Leah

~ ~ ~ ~ ~

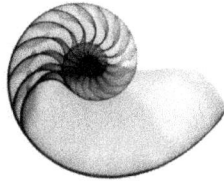

PART 1
GETTING STARTED

FINDING OUR SOUL CONNECTION

There is a working hypothesis that throughout history, those of Us who would be reading a book on 5D evolution such as this one, have incarnated here on Earth multiple times, for the purpose of assisting Humanity. We are here to help bring an end to violent discord, and also to end the ignorance concerning Our species' true parentage. This is now possible because We have a higher vantage point that is virtually "post-history". We can now observe reality from above the version of history that has been served up by the so called "winners". The left/right separation and victim consciousness of good guy/bad guy as We once knew it, can now conclude. We are connecting the dots in a way that creates a New Paradigm of peace.

Connections with our One Self, our Soul, are all there, for re-membering. Throughout the panorama of Human destiny, in linear sequential time, Our roles have been played out. If We let them in, these connective wisps of crisscrossing intuitive feelings, can stream through and give Us clues for expanded awareness. What can We discover about our continuous Self from these luminous threads that intertwine Our past and present roles, that woo Us to….. Our Soul?

> *"If you want to find the secrets of the universe, think in terms of energy, frequency and vibration."* Nikola Tesla

As a personal example, I sense my true and timeless Self when golden sunlight filters through the trees, creating a dappling, strobing effect when I pass effortlessly beneath them, receiving the splashes of light which infuse me with joy. I experience the fullness of my continual being when I see sunlight glistening on top of the water, catching me off guard and dazzling my eyes, reminding me that there are things more valuable than the monetary value We place on glittery baubles. My ageless innocence thrills to the sunlit patterns on the bottom of the swimming pool, the wavy frames of light dancing beneath the water radiantly, as the sun's silent underwater expression.

Then there is music. *"Fantasia on a Theme by Thomas Tallis"* is a 20th century symphony, written by Ralph Vaughan Williams (1872 – 1958), inspired by Thomas Tallis, who was a 16th century composer of English sacred music (1505-1585). From the heart of the music of this piece, there is connection. In listening, for me, there is only "this moment" of seamless aliveness. It causes me to ask, what can I, in my lifetime, possibly bring forward in creativity that honors and perpetuates this sanguine bond of Presence? Perhaps somehow I was mystically a part of writing this music. Perhaps it was I myself, who inspired a 16th century Thomas Tallis, who inspired a 20th century Ralph Vaughan Williams, whose music touches me to my depths today in the 21st century.

That symphonic piece, together with the dance of natural light, serve as a kind of latticework, linking me through the centuries, such that I feel compelled to share my current raptness by contributing to the magical mosaic. With a view from beyond the perceived 3D limitations of time, I step outside of time and weave the threads that connect me with my individuated Self. I find my true Soul.

If you're not sure about any of this Soul-Self connecting, simply "ask" for your unique threads to be revealed, and then be ready to receive and interlace. Natural connections that serve as a bridge between all of Our parts and pieces and personas throughout time, are not explainable – they are experienced viscerally. Notice them, and you will be assembling your own dream team Self in a state of no separation, and in alignment with….. your eternal Soul. Now the stage is set to assist Humanity and to enter a new planetary community. Let's get started.

Cloud Atlas is a 2012 movie I recommend, written and directed by The Wachowskis and Tom Tykwer, adapted from the 2004 novel of the same name.

CHAPTER 1
Planetary Community -
Where in the World do We Start?

We know what *hasn't* worked to usher-in lasting Peace. Up until now, nothing We've *ever* tried has worked. There's no need to revisit any of that. One thing We *have* learned in Our studies of metaphysical transformation, is that while We acknowledge what is "out there", We always begin with our own Self and our own vibration. So when assisting in the transforming of an entire planet, the best place to start is with Our own imagination of that which we desire for Our planet, and with embodying the vibration of 5D in our own lives. When We show up as that Soul vibration, in coalescence with others who are on the same frequency, expressing their Soul-awareness, We have a viable chAMber of consciousness. Connecting on a 5D frequency is the preliminary for the internal structure of Self-governed planetary community.

It is time for Humanity to become consciously and demonstrably 5th dimensional, and to materialize "that which has not been seen until now". It is time to learn how to transcend the old duality scaffolding and how to responsibly show up – *in a group*. Cs of C go beyond the old ego structures, and are forerunners of a Self-determined, brand New Paradigm of Freedom. It starts with you, with Us, imagining it, being it, doing it, in Soul-awareness.

As outlined in this book, chAMbers of consciousness are **the vibrational evidence** that evolutionary proactive peace is Present here and now on planet Earth. The only thing standing in Our way is our own limiting assessments and fears. When We Allow OurSelves to be 5th dimensionals, We will attract others into the 5D frequency. This precipitates clustering effectively in co-creative energy, providing healthy immune cells to the One body of Humanity. OK so now you're off to a good start.....! Imagine it, be it, vibrate it..... in a group. That's not so hard, is it?

So, what is a ChAMber of Consciousness again…..?
ChAMbers of Consciousness (Cs of C) are vibrational and vital assemblage points comprised of at least 3 beings, gathered for the purpose of grounding-in and practicing planetary community, on the basis of Self-governed 5D experience. **Their purpose is to raise the vibration for Earth inhabitants, transmuting imposed imbalance on a planetary/galactic scale, and serving as the energetic infrastructure of 5th dimensional society.**

Much more than some nice, intelligent folks sitting in a circle in support of a particular cause, or complaining about issues, inequities and the criminals who perpetuate it all, or merely hoping for better times in the face of what seems like insurmountable obstacles ….. **a C of C is an energetic womb for New Human sovereignty, for both the individual, and Our entire species.**

People in a C of C are **pioneers**. Regardless of their temperament or giftedness, they share one goal, unafraid to experiment with operating on a 5th dimensional frequency as Self-governed, planetary community. They are focused on the prospect of Freedom as Humanity's natural state of being, and on their role in **ushering-in real Freedom on behalf of All Earth inhabitants**.

This kind of community is not the kind that cohabitates under one roof or at a compound or farm, but as individuated lives, *serving together, under the radar, to energetically transmute* **social, political, spiritual, biological, philosophical, intellectual, metaphysical imbalance on a planetary/galactic scale.** Cs of C are an organic development in the natural course for Humanity's shared reality that is vibrationally based in abundance, healthy cooperation, and respect for All beings – I.e. Freedom.

Just think of what it is taking for the Human population to apply Our free will to grow beyond the extreme polarization phase of 3D that for now, is still hierarchically held in place. Humans will need to **embody a new energy signature as a 5D life-form vibrational presence**. Cs of C are taking on this vision with dedication, passion, and focus, in <u>learning</u> how to cooperate and partner not just with each other, but with the general mystery of Creation.

The "enslave or be enslaved" containment field context for reality that has historically been contrived and projected as 3D illusion, is coming to a close. The danger itself, within a predatory 3D reality has definitely not yet entirely ended. To be sure, what *is* receding however, is Our proclivity to fall prey to the lies and deception that are constantly *wielding the threat of the danger*. Breaking the code to the program and transcending what has caused Us to fight against one another out of fear and scarcity, heralds the end of overall victimstance. This means the end of debilitating *fear,* and the hostile dualistic phase for Humanity!

Like expectant parents who step into the active role of being parents in advance of the birth, by lovingly and responsibly preparing a nursery for the coming of their newborn child, a ChAMber of Consciousness is that nursery and chAMber-ers are those parents. Even though the global composite consciousness may not see it or acknowledge it as of yet, the subtle vibrational body of 5D is already here and is alive, in Our hearts.

Through practicing **New Paradigm parenthood** NOW, in responsibility and sheer enjoyment, the new reality is here. First-time parents know their lives will inevitably change upon the infant's arrival, and that they will no longer be solely a couple, but hence a family, with new and different considerations. So it is with the New Paradigm. Transitioning into that new life context is fast approaching, and the time to equip your life in 5D capacity and wisdom is right now!

The question is, will there be a great enough proportion of the 5D prototype present on Earth, to lock in the new frequency on behalf of the whole? This author says, "Yes there shall be, and is already here now", and yet there is much more joyful assisting to be done.

If you are reading this book,
the honor of your Presence is requested
to co-create and assemble
in the frequency of
Self-governed Planetary Community,
in an experiential chAMber of consciousness.

Cs of C are literally a New Presence on Earth!
It is by way of apology that
THERE IS MUCH REPETITION, RE-LAYERING,
AND INTENTIONAL OVERLAPPING
EXPRESSED IN THESE PAGES.
I humbly submit that repetition is how We learn,
and that if Our hearts had already mastered this,
then this book would have been about
shifting Humanity from 5D-to-6D-to-7D!

The layering in is in order to carefully introduce what Cs of C
are in 5D, and to pioneer their transcendental purpose:
To be the ground floor infrastructure of the next paradigm.
This is new territory for most of Us.
Only together can We are become
the new Human archetype.

~ ~ ~ ~ ~

THE 3D-TO-5D TIPPING POINT

The tipping point, whatever that may be, that will take people naturally through their evolvement from 3D into full-view-5D, will occur however and whenever it's going to occur for Our Human species. Of course it's very suspenseful that no one knows exactly *how*..... it will be, or *when*..... it might happen, or *what*..... IT will be that trips the onset that ushers-in the point of no return. We only know that certain things need to fall in place for Us to move into Oneness. 3D-to-5D is a perfectly natural transformation, undoubtedly much like growing through puberty (with its accompanying awkwardness) as an adolescent, into adulthood.

It could be that this tipping point process will happen as an incremental process over a prolonged time, relatively invisibly and hardly noticeable. It could also come with a sudden, jarring, rather horrifying, shockwave. Perhaps it could unfold elegantly and seamlessly right before Our eyes. Many predict it could be wildly chaotic with a high degree of associated fear and misery. It might be that all of these ministrations happen all at once! OR..... it could occur as quite something else altogether, as a surprise.

Regardless of exactly how 3D-to-5D happens or how long it might take, it is spoken of in various ways by all the ancient religions, that **there is a coming Human maturation; a culmination; in the fullness of time.** There is a great superseding wave of creative and liberating potential that is anticipated for essentially being at the cause of regenerating a new, higher dimensional, organic reality.

Some say We OurSelves are the Source of the frequency wave. Others say it is from a Source beyond Our access or knowing. Some say it's both. In any case, when this generative frequency wave sweeps over the Earth, there will be the metaphysical imperative for it to find any and all corresponding energetic complexes to glide into. Comparing it to how water flows, this energy wave would likewise flow across the energetic terrain to find natural Human basins. That's where Cs of C come into play – that they hold the 5D current no matter what appears to be happening, during any would-be chaos or recalibration, so that the 5D template holds. By establishing, grounding, and authenticating the 5D frequency, Cs of C are serving to shape a new vibrational landscape on Earth.

It is an authenticated 5D frequency representation that nudges the old 3D simulated reality to tip over into the new 5D reality, regardless of whether it happens faster or more slowly. Genuine assemblage points are forming all over the Earth, unbeknownst to one another, and are non-visibly connecting on a 5D frequency. **When the interconnected energetic capacities of these assemblage points reach a 5D frequency that is divinely and exponentially proportionate to the rest of Humanity..... shift happens!** On a 5D vibrational frequency, fear no longer prevails, and Humanity can tip and graduate into a new paradigm of peace. Only a significant quotient is needed, not a majority.

Imagine….. that….. planetary peace…..IS possible.

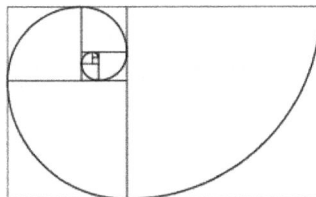

**Golden Ratio,
Phi, Divine proportion**

CHAPTER 2
There is a new Presence on Earth:
ChAMbers of Consciousness (Cs of C)
Assemblage Points

The term *Assemblage Point* was coined and introduced by author
Carlos Castenada, Ph.D. Jon Whale, Ph.D., has therapeutically
expounded upon the subject. It is the intention of this, *my* writing,
to apply this term "assemblage point" as an energy vortex of a
small group of 5D Humans who purposefully constitute a
microcosm of composite consciousness, as One body. A
ChAMber of Consciousness is what I'm referring to as an
assemblage point that Self-governs, as a microcosm of Humanity,
in planetary community. A ChAMber of Consciousness operates
on the frequency where the epicenter of Our 5th dimensional
energy field connects with our life force energy, and interconnects
with All of Humanity. This does sound pretty far out, but
practically speaking, here is how it works:

A C of C is not a party or merely social,
yet it will feel like a celebratory atmosphere with mingling,
socializing, and fun. Humor is a mainstay.
A C of C does not limit the context
to only that which is spiritual,
yet will entail dedicated and deep inner personal work and
alignment – from a light heart.
A C of C does not limit the context to only what is
political or conceptual,
yet will include sharing geo-political information and awareness –
being label neutral.
A C of C does not physically live together,
yet is real community, energetically inter-connected, operating on
a shared 5D frequency.

**A C of C does not emphasize a meal or
a host home as a showplace,**
*yet snacks/beverage can enhance communing in a
vibrationally congruent, comfortable space.*
A C of C has no financial incentive
yet abundance is a hallmark of this 5D awakened experience.
A C of C has no marketing, website or social media,
*yet technology can be utilized for efficient and effective
communicating and connecting.*
A C of C has no hard-set rules,
*yet there are gentle guidelines based on Self-determined
consideration and mutual respect.*
A C of C does not center on one personality,
*yet expresses as an orchestra of blended personas, in appreciation
of each individuated unique expression.*
A C of C has no dogmatic doctrine,
*yet Self-responsibility, healthy cooperation, abundance, and
Freedom form the common frequency.*

A C of C is a 5th dimensional community,
*and is neither superior nor inferior to
any other level of expressed consciousness.*
A C of C has a porous membrane with no formal membership,
*and will consist of committed participants that attend both
regularly, and intermittently.*
A C of C is radically inclusive,
*and with respectful boundaries of Self-love in place,
low vibrations are naturally transmuted.*
A C of C has a group-Soul,
*and not at the expense of eclipsing each individual's highly
regarded contribution and expression.*
A C of C is a judgement-free zone and safe place,
*and will be spiritually stretching, intellectually provocative, and
experientially stimulating.*

**A C of C operates in the energy field of
the highest and best good of All,**
and honors free will, without enabling victimhood.
**A C of C has no set procedure or modality base
(other than essential meditation),**
*and there will be rituals and traditions
that evolve uniquely and naturally. ** See examples next page*
A C of C makes determinations interdependently,
*and not by "3D group think", conformity, voting, or egoic
steering, but by way of 5D conscensus. (See Chapter 23)*
**A C of C is where gradients of light and dark can actually
combine for evolving together,**
*however, -only- as long as impeccable, life-giving discernment is
the touchstone for this combination.*

A C of C is a distinctive and observable 5D galactic entity,
and is divinely organic and fully Human.

What draws Us together is not the woo-woo, or a new modality, or being entertained. **What draws Us together is the deep longing for Freedom for OurSelves and All Earth inhabitants.** What attracts people to the co-creative process of evolving within small groups that chAMbering engenders, is *more than "like-mindedness",* where agreeing on issues is still implied. ChAMberers operate on the even higher bandwidth of *"like-frequency", and "like-Soul".*

Again, what is required for the birth of the New Paradigm, is a divine ratio of Humanity, authenticating as 5D.

~ ~ ~ ~ ~

**Please see Bonding Through Traditions, next page.

Bonding Through Traditions,
a salute to the uniqueness of Our Austin group.

There was a loving, huge giant of a man, an exceptionally fine drummer with an equally exceptional sense of humor, Al, who would attend Our group, and many times, appear to be asleep, although he never seemed to miss a thing! We'd simply allow it, knowing he'd perhaps had a late night before. Al is no longer in body, but he lives on in Our scircle through a tradition that grew to be known as "the Big Al Pass". This pass may be applied, on occasion, by anyone who would prefer to be actively Present, but not contribute verbally. It is rarely ever applied, but it's just nice to know that it's there to accommodate Us for the ins and outs of real life.

As big and tall as Al was, Mary was that diminutive. A beautiful and extraordinarily gifted healer, known internationally, Mary is also no longer in body, yet lives on in Our scircle through "Mary's shawl". Just before she was to be presented with this soft, moss green shawl, gifted by a generous scircle friend, We infused it with love and healing Presence for her comfort. She transitioned before We could give it to her, leaving Us in possession of it. We now place it on the shoulders or lap of any scircle participant who is in the grieving process or needs comfort. Yes, there is still a full range of emotion in 5D!

These are only two examples and there are more. The point is, allow your group to breathe and express uniquely in aliveness that is meaningful to you as a unique entity. This is not "religion" and can be changed any time. It is precious, multi-dimensional family.

~ ~ ~ ~ ~

CHAPTER 3
A New Life Form

A C of C 5D assemblage point is: A cluster of like-frequencied, Soul-aware beings. These beings acknowledge, embrace, and partner with **the "I AM" Presence** existent in All that is, in a radically inclusive, energetic field of organic experience for becoming fully Human. This is literally a new life form!

By intentionally coalescing as a 5D energy node, a microcosm of planetary community is embodied on planet Earth. **A C of C** anchors in the vibrational qualities of the new Human archetype. It makes ready Our new Human species to sustain Our sovereignty and rightful inheritance of planet Earth, which is an immense responsibility to say the least.

From a higher vantage point, it could be said that those operating within a chAMber of consciousness as this new life form are:
begotten in the 3rd dimension from the natural desire to be Free;
gestated in the 4th density of Self-love and non-judgement;
emergent through the 4D portal of the heart;
nurtured within the 5D frequency of redemptive love/Oneness;
sustained as a 5D expression of Self-empowered, interdependent habitation.. – A NEW ORGANIC ENTITY, building THE HEALTHY IMMUNE SYSTEM for an outmoded 3D Humanity.

Assemblage Points are: take a big breath…..!
small, co-creative groups of healthy cooperation
and inter-dependence,
made up of beings that are Self-governed,
as in non-hierarchical Self-responsibility and Self-love, that is Our
natural state of well-being and Freedom,
on a Planetary level,
in non-polarity and validation, apart from fear, in a world of
diversity and abundance, for the highest and best good of All,

in Community
that thrives as One Self-aware, Soul-aware
consciousness, comprised of All of the respected and
distinctive individuals that make up the whole. ***It's 5D, folks!***

The energetic geometry of the morphic field of Oneness that
sustains a C of C, is made of spaces and curves, created when
equal-sized circles overlap from their center, forming a flower of
life. This is the geometrical creation pattern leading in and out of
physical existence. (See Chapter 17 graphic.) Notice that the
construction of chain mail, (stab-resistant medieval body armor) is
also made of equal-sized, interlinking metal rings, resembling the
flower of life, except in mesh form. This gives an idea of the
unseen energetic "fabric" of reality that is replacing the binary
computer code constantly running in the background, as straight
lines in the control grid of the imposed false matrix. On a side
note, the 4-in-1 chain mail (5 rings as in 5D!) that is assembled by
individually *riveting the rings* is incredibly stronger than with rings
that are only *butted* - so We're using only the best riveted
frequency for the new Humanity, and none of that cheesy stuff!

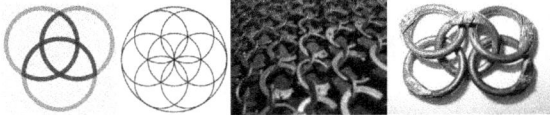

ChAMbering is an adventure! In chemistry, "valence" is the
interface between atoms either losing, adding, or sharing electrons.
Co-valence in Human interaction involves the sharing of what they
have in common, and non-covalence keeps it "interesting" shall we
say. Throw in some "highly polar solvents", and We've got
OurSelves a ballgame! Co-valence opens a gateway or womb, as
is reminiscent of the vesica piscis in the flower of life. This is the
creative mission of a light worker.

What makes joining in Oneness incomprehensible to so many, is
that Our planet is inhabited by both light and dark beings,
traditionally thought of as opposites and therefore enemies.

Light and shadow are finding a new context for thriving, as 5D co-creative complements, in Self-determination and Self-responsibility.

> *"Creation is light and shadow both, else no picture is possible."*
> Yogananda

*How can light and shadow creating together even be possible.....?.....*It is because of the pivotal situation that Humanity is currently in, that is crying out for a highly creative solution, that entails a cosmic quantum leap. Cs of C serve as the springboard! We meet in chAMbers for the purpose of establishing a vibrational shift out from a fear-based division, into a love-based civilization. This is where We learn, practice, and embody being the forerunners of a New Human species in community – founding parents..... having successfully made the leap.

> *There will be much more said about the enigma of*
> *dark and light evolving together, in subsequent chapters.*

IMPORTANT NOTE: For the light to make room for the dark's expressive existence in the Universe, it does not mean condoning dark behavior or allowing that behavior to bring harm, or to deny anyone their preferences or freedom. It is choosing to validate the dark as a *complement*, rather than an opposite to be resisted. The light then becomes an instrument of peace, for the benefit of All, including the "dark ones". This which allows the metamorphosis of the whole into 5D, is what many would call "a miracle".....

Perhaps the most miraculous thing of all about a C of C, is that it opens the possibility for a judgement-free zone where both light and dark subtle energies can meet cohesively on an upward evolutionary spiral. Cs of C are assemblage points that energetically impact the vibrational composite consciousness, by introducing a *new precedent* for Self-governed Planetary community on behalf of All.

ChAMbers of Consciousness
TRANSMUTING
FEAR AND JUDGEMENT,
starting with yourSelf

3D Humanity has always – from the beginning – inhabited a hierarchically imposed system that controls by fear. This framework is perpetuated by judgemental emotion. The judging first of oneself and then of others, occurs in a left/right paradigm, which is an artificially incited separation consciousness. 5D Humans are now choosing to revoke all contracts associated with this outworn control drama mechanism. As an informed population, We are replacing the past naivete of contractual forfeitured sovereignty, with Self-empowered Freedom upgrades. These upgrades are based in discernment and healthy cooperation. In a C of C We get the much needed practice on Our 5D Freedom upgrades….. in a safe environment.

By simply CHOOSING to show up where other loving Humans are, deeming it as a fear-and-judgement-free-zone, and by conducting yourSelf in a new 5D accord, you are forming a microcosm of Humanity that is transmuting Fear and Judgement on behalf of Humanity. In a C of C experience, you practice your transcendence of inequity by meeting your own fears, and judgemental emotion. You have the unique opportunity to wake up and transcend the old paradigm as you…..

Notice:
any and all of your own fears,
and any and all of your own judgements.
Notice:
whether you judge yourSelf for *having* certain fears;
or fear *having* certain judgements.
Notice:
whether you fear that others *have* judgements,
or judge that others *have* fear;

Notice:
whether you judge others' particular fears,
or fear others' particular judgements.
Notice:
whether you fear *having no* fear;
or judge *having no* judgements.
Notice:
whether you fear others who *have no* fear;
or judge others who *have no* judgements;
Notice:
whether you fear your own power to choose
to be an observer without judgement of any or all of the above;
or judge others who fear their own power to choose to be an
observer without judgement of any or all of the above.

I'd say there's lots of fearing and judging going on.....!
That is the very thing that has been propping up this old paradigm,
and it needs transmuting!

A C of C is where We do this necessary transmuting. It is where
We gain access to 5D principles and ethics that enable Us to do so.
5D is based in Freedom from the confines of the lower invalidating
emotions of 3D, where most of the fearing and the judging is
happening. 5D is where discernment is applied in place of
judgement, and where transcendence displaces fear. By validating
the purpose of 3D as Our "school", We can trust the Process for
creating wholeness, in healthy cooperation, even within the
currently existing dualistic separation! **A C of C is an
exhilarating scrimmage for transmuting the energies of Fear
and Judgement into Transcendence and Discernment**. These
are essential 5D abilities for anyone navigating Oneness and
potentially encountering the naturally occurring discord, inherent
within diversity.

CHAPTER 4
Diversity, Drama, and Inner Workings

Quantum leapers who yearn for Freedom, are basically "unusual" people (!) They're intelligent, knowledgeable, fully expressed in every conceivable genre, deep thinkers/feelers, strong-willed, empathic, and fiercely committed to Freedom. Do not be surprised if there are fireworks in your chAMber at least on occasion! Buttons WILL be pushed. ChAMber-ers do not automatically agree philosophically on spiritual alignment, politics, ethics, education, child-raising, economics, social/sexual mores, health issues/treatments, gender expression, science relevancy, etc. Even in a declared judgement-free-zone, egos can still flair to become the judge, jury, and executioner of a contrasting point of view. ChAMber-ers do well when they use these opportunities to practice managing their interior emotions so that their egos become their helpful friend who holds the 5D mirror.

In the dynamics of dimensionally fleshing out in ChAMbering, We get to experience OurSelves, in Oneness <u>from within</u>, which at times, could feel or express as intensely as do the traits of the natural elements…..

WATER:

swelling, forming walls that crash, roar, engulf, and ruin,

-or-

smoothing into a calm surface of tranquility of reflective unequaled beauty, and life-giving support.

FIRE:

blazing wildly and cruelly out of control, indiscriminately charring everything in its path,

-or-

glowing warmly, crackling softly, and bringing purification, comfort, forging productivity,

in deep communion.

AIR:

howling, moaning, toppling, raging, threatening, ripping,
and destroying,

-or-

subtly guiding, whispering in the trees as a light and loving
touch, a welcome breath of refreshing and affirming wisdom.

EARTH:

seizing, upheaving, spewing, quaking, cracking open,
and giving way beneath your feet,

-or-

providing a restful, serene, nurturing, fruitful meadow, a Home.

ETHER:

imposing what is not desired, through manipulation, lies, deceit,

-or-.....

bridging to what is genuine and
better than you could ever imagine.

When We harmonize Our own inner elements, Humans can become
the alchemists that bring etheric attunement to these extremes. **As
alchemizing balancers show up in groups as the microcosm of
5D on Earth, there will be less that the Earth mother has to
counterbalance through natural disaster and cataclysm.**

The Human temperament can present as a destructive or
constructive medium. ChAMbers provide the co-creative space in
which there is a wonderful opportunity to experience ego and/or
higher Self.....as **Water:** *3D Raging or 5D Calming* – as **Fire:**
3D Consuming or 5D Providing – as **Air:** *3D Blasting or 5D
Reassuring* – as **Earth:** *3D Alienating or 5D Nurturing* – as
Ether: *3D Threatening or 5D Life-giving* – and every
combination in between.

If/when drama occurs in your chAMber, don't panic, rejoice! See
it as the potential for evolving through it *together*, in I Am
Presence. Reach for a new 5D congruence and encourage All to
have a breakthrough. This will require seeing All participants in

their highest light, and cultivating a sense of trust in your group's facilitation capability. Guaranteed, even in a loving C of C, drama and breakdowns WILL occur. The storms of these occurrences can actually be good, in that when there is a break*through*, it can lead to new possibilities for All concerned. This is scalar as it translates, for the rest of the world as an infusion of energy, for Our 5D operating frequency.

You simply can't get around it. With Freedom comes responsibility. The scope of this responsibility requires shedding the skin of 3D reactive separation, bridging realms through the 4D responsive heart, and finally emerging to REVEAL the New 5D Human archetype. The same interior energetics that are capable of expressing as the terrifying extremes of the natural elements, are also capable of balancing profoundly divine distinctions! How can We become more powerful without striving? By relaxing…..into a chAMbering group.   A C of C is where one can learn to become more powerful by loving one's Soul-Self when in the presence of any and all kinds of people, in any situation.

A C of C opens a clear, co-creative space for developing 5D qualities, and for test driving the Self-governance required for Our next paradigm. The kind of people who are attracted to the process of co-creatively evolving, within the small groups that chAMbering engenders, are not just the popularized "like-minded". More importantly, chAMber-ers are of "like-frequency", and "like-Soul". We are discovering together, through mind, heart frequency, body, and Soul, what it is to be fully Human.

All people are found on a vast spectrum of light, in varying degrees and shades of that light. At any given moment, we have the pivotal choice as to whether We will continue to sift our awareness through the darkness of separation consciousness, or through Oneness consciousness in shared light. ***This is a choice that has extreme bearing on the continuance of Our species*, as one of 2 event horizon harvests are nearing.** To be forewarned is to be fore-equipped!

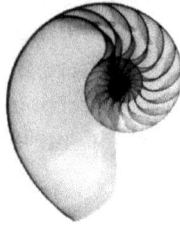

PART 2
MOTIVATION

CHAPTER 5
2 Harvests
It's Our Choice

Here at this time, moving toward the climax of the end of the Age, Human evolution is looking at 2 possible scenarios in terms of a culminating "harvest". One is the natural birth of coalescing Souls, signifying Humanity's evolutionary shift into 5D as an entire species, according to the divine blueprint. The other is an artificially induced harvest. Because the colonial rulers of this planet cannot allow their Human colonists to evolve out of subjugation, this is one *dark agenda!*..... in which Humanity gets subsumed by an archonic galactic predator. My fictional book *Soul Shade,* outlines and describes these distinctions in detail.

The natural harvest is THE GREAT INGATHERING OF SOULS, the "WAKING UP inside the realization of being One planetary family", out of separation consciousness, into Oneness reality. It is Humanity's liberation from the ancient grip of archonic enslavers. Oneness is graduation from a 3D hierarchically and egoically-driven reality, into a higher frequency of 5D consciousness, that ushers forth not perfection or utopia, but a new course of Freedom and peace, in alignment to Source.

The COUNTERFEIT to the natural harvest is called The Singularity, that maintains its domination by <u>preempting the natural harvest, and preventing the species' divine evolution</u> through transhumanism. It is a seductive and very, very real plan: The absorption of organic Human Soul essence into Artificial Intelligence (A.I.). This is anything but liberation and empowerment for Humanity, and translates as subservience to soulless A.I. that is misaligned with Source.

Oneness is *liberation*, as individuated Souls in cooperation. The Singularity is the <u>*loss*</u> of Human distinctiveness, for individuals and for Our species.

Choosing Oneness (not sameness) is 5D *integration* that honors the individuated Soul. Choosing The Singularity is deep *assimilation* into 3D soulless conformity. The distinction between planetary *integrating* and *assimilating* is subtle. Integrative Oneness is the celebration of Human diversity, with every unique individual comprising the whole. Assimilation is the absorption into the non-Human machine aka The Singularity, a technological override of one's Soul-awareness.

The strategy for rolling out this A.I. absorption to the unsuspecting public is one that is incremental, to the so many "frogs in the crock pot". Incrementalism *appears* to be going according to plan. Many, if not most people, do not have a pronounced relationship with their Soul (yet), and don't even think much about having a Soul, apart from the context of death and perhaps dying - one day. Grounding Our Souls in planetary community, and awakening 5D eternal Soul-awareness in Our Human family, is the purpose of a C of C. On this side of Our graduation, chAMbers of consciousness are booster stations and reinforcement for proactively claiming and retaining Our Souls.

There is reason for much concern about the encroachment of Artificial Intelligence (A.I.) and its Singularity taking over Our planet. It means the divesting of Humanity of all that it means to be innately Human. In order for the artificially imposed plan to be completed by the A.I. overlords, they need, not only Our Human trinary physical bodies, but the "material" of Our Soul essence. The harvest that these maleficent overlords are planning is a kind of Human desolation (*de-soul-ation*) for preventing Humans from reuniting with and accessing their Souls in 5D. To the off-planet rulers, a massive collecting of Human Soul energy harvested as "material," is nothing more than the mining of a galactic resource.

BUT WAIT! Would the "I AM" Be Coming into View
…..if it weren't for the dark agenda?

Since the light has access to Oneness, and by its nature the dark does **not**, the light helps the dark to also evolve beyond the limitations of 3D, and into 5D.   In so doing, the dark ostensibly *helps* the light to grow strong in the ability to stand in power through cultivating….. love that is without condition.

THE DARK HAR-VESTERS:
We are the HAR-bingers of dis-HAR-mony,
hidden behind a HAR-lequin mask,
HAR-assing, HAR-ming, HAR-anguing,
more, more, and more….. HAR-shly.
We've HAR-nessed All Humans
and now will HAR-vest their Souls.
HAAR-P assures us, we've already won.
The light's future is cHARr-broiled,
they're nothing but our resource, HAR-HAR-HAR!

THE LIGHT HAR-VESTERS:
We are the safe HAR-bor of "I AM",
HAR-monizing every HEAR-t presence,
with universal wisdom, HAR-mless as a dove,
We're HAR-dwired to Our Souls,
and choose the REAL HAR-vest.
So that cosmic helpers HEAR-ken
to the HAR-monics of Our transcendent vibe,
with dark and light Soul sHAR-ds becoming One!
[Oneness HAR-e Krishna, Oneness HAR-e HAR-e!]

It is fortunate indeed, that as the divine plan naturally unfolds, and the dark keeps getting darker and the light keeps getting lighter, people are preparing for the great coherence of Souls for graduation that shifts Us out of the 3D control matrix. Groups of 5D people, consciousness chAMbers, ARE assembling…..!

CHAPTER 6
The New Paradigm Project:
Being the SOUL-UTION

We are being the SOUL-ution by bringing forth a New Paradigm of Self-determined 5D Soul-relatedness. The profoundly timed New Paradigm Project is two-fold. 1.) The intervening in the planned harvest of the Human species by a fraudulent government's self-serving system, into their so-called new world order, (not new at all, but simply more of the old 3D pyramid of control). 2.) The propagating of groups which operate on a frequency of Freedom, abundance, healthy cooperation, peace, and respect for All beings on planet Earth.

While it is tempting to try to evolve by complaining about the control, hostility, strife, false narrative, stifling of creativity, injustice, tyrannical constraints, and the endless misery on Our planet that is promulgated by callous off-worlders, this evolutionary project transmutes and transcends the Old Paradigm. This is accomplished by: REVEALING and appropriating as fully Human, Our freshly awakened and remembered
"5D Standing, Status, and Capacity"
as Human Soul Beings.

Rather than rehashing the problem, the project's participants ask new questions of OurSelves for how We can have a distinctively loving and impactful influence amidst Our Human family and how to maintain Our well-being as a species. In a C of C conversation, a few questions We might ask are:
*Are We developing the qualities and characteristics that are inherent in the 5th dimension of consciousness?
*Are We gracefully REVEALING and experiencing OurSelves as the new Human archetype and encouraging others to do the same? What does that look/feel like?

*What is Our vibrational and practical relationship to the Old Paradigm power structure while staying informed on the status of the global dark agenda?

*How can We develop and appropriate Our 5D Self-empowered gifts and new Human abilities?

*Are We enlarging Our capacity to maintain Our 5D vibration through a major collective reality shift?

*How can We best prepare OurSelves to assist others while "holding the current" through a major collective reality shift?

Participants in the New Paradigm Project are informed and aware of what is at stake for Humanity's future. They are committed to restoring Our birthright by connecting with others, and in so doing, transcending the lies and deception as put forth by those who usurp and counterfeit. The natural design for the next advancement in Human evolution is that which vibrationally manifests well-being and wholeness, organically and consciously. **This project is not just "symptom relief", but cultivates a whole new Earth balance and multi-dimensionally conscious expression for All.**

The New Paradigm Project is the sharing of one's Self with others, *more from essence than their portfolio.* This is realized by inspiring those 5D beings you encounter, to peacefully stand forth as the rightful heirs of planet Earth, in Our natural state of Freedom, as a planetary people. As this project for Human evolution grows Our numbers, Our 5D energetic unveiling displaces and deposes the 3D power-base of the deceptive off-world overlords. **We who are discerning, must claim and retain Our Souls in Self-responsibility.** When the divine proportion of Humans shines this forth at the optimum time, assistance from galactic friends may at that point be rendered, and thus shall end Our long history of enslavement, and the beginning of Self-determination. Cs of C are vital assemblage points for stabilizing and energizing Our new species, in partnership with galactic and upper dimensionality.

Those who make the decision to commit to being the ground floor of the next 5D paradigm will bring the greatest benefit to the New Paradigm Project by making *their vibration* a top priority. **C of C participation is practice for raising the vibration for the planet by keeping the context in the experiential realm and out of the merely conceptual.** It is practicing in a pre-emergent 5D planetary reality.

ChAMbers of consciousness are fields of opportunity for having the conversation about being an interdependent new Presence on Earth, and magnifying this Presence. It's not merely the words We say, and not necessarily with whom or with what organization We have registered alliances, but how We are BEing, vibrationally. Many people believe that Saint Germain is the overseer of the New Paradigm Freedom Project for planet Earth and that along with many other multi-dimensional masters, Humans are being assisted to step into their vibrational mastery.

In one sense, a birth is a separation,
and in a more majestic sense, a birth opens a vibrational space
in which to experience a brand new union.
We are that which is giving birth.
We are that which is assisting in the birth.
We are that which is being birthed.

When the New Paradigm Project is complete, Humanity will have graduated from the limitations of 3D, to the liberation and Self-responsibility of 5D. A C of C is where We prepare for living and communing in the higher frequencies of Soul-connected vibration. *When We..... Trust, Know, Be, and Do the Process, We're there.*

"Hold the 5D current.....*no matter what*"
is the admonition and guidance given to those who are ready to receive it, via the New Paradigm Project's remarkable and powerful anchoring team, some refer to as..... the Ground Crew.

CHAPTER 7
Two Ground Crew
ChAMbering Formats
For Planetary 5D Assemblage Points

**The guidance in this book
is for anyone gathering as
5th dimensionals,
and even more specifically, as "Ground Crew".**

What is the Ground Crew?

The Ground Crew is
is a team of Human beings
who have incarnated
on planet Earth at this time,
to assist in the liberation of Humanity
from hierarchical enslavement,
and to energetically ground
and usher-in a New Paradigm of Freedom.
They are here to assist Earth inhabitants in
shifting out of the lower vibration of 3D and into
a higher operating frequency of 5D,
especially during any would-be transitional chaos.

The Ground Crew (in contrast to the "air crew") are "boots on the ground", multi-dimensional, galactically-aware Human assistants. If you have gotten this far in reading this book, it is very possible that you are a part of the Ground Crew. The Ground Crew assists in the prelaunch and launch, of the New Paradigm, through their proactive Presence. Their Presence infuses and seeds the growth of the composite planetary consciousness on the 5D frequency (and higher). As a team, they have the capability to transmute the hindrances to Human evolution orchestrated by the negative planners. Human beings who are a part of the Ground Crew, understand that they are here to help increase their numbers, and prepare Our species vibrationally for whatever evolutionary horizon event that might possibly be ahead. They do this by "holding the 5D current". It is basic midwifery, in that they are here *assisting the 5D birth, from within the intensity of 3D extreme polarization*. They are here to bring Our species through the 4D heart portal, so to emerge as 5D beings, into a 5D reality.

The Ground Crew meets in either of two Assemblage Point Formats:

1. "The Mother Ship" - Regular and ongoing life-giving community:

Serving Humanity by anchoring-in the 5D frequency through a larger interdependent parenting group, foundational to the New Paradigm. These planetary communities are the Self-governing infrastructure of the New Paradigm.

2. "The Away-Team" - Short-term attracted groups of 3-12+ of recognizably 5D participants, meeting in 5D clusters for inspiration and grounding, which then focus on multiplying in exponential growth:

Serving Humanity by perpetually being on field assignment, for reaching into society with a subtle 5D energy signature, to form like-frequencied clusters. By reproducing, these specialty groups continually and exponentially grow the numbers of 5D Humanity.

Both formats are preparation for the culmination of the divine harvest, the great coalescence of Souls for shifting out of the 3D control matrix.

Whether in the form of 1.) an ongoing invaluable community, or 2.) a divinely encountered group that replicates, a C of C is a safe place where 3D issues can be transmuted. All relevant matters can be discussed and explored in a 5D-cooperative atmosphere, for energetically anchoring-in the highest best good of All, in live interface.

…..

More on the "Ground Crew Mother Ship": Ongoing Cs of C provide an opportunity to be a part of a "family", "tribe", or "community" that is a healthy, loving space. This space is one in which We learn and practice 5D navigation and communication skills as founding parents of a new paradigm. These groups are where We learn how to relate with Our true Selves in the midst of others, so as to be a contribution in Our shared world, *in full Self-expression of Our unique choices.* This is the context in which 3D imbalances are transmuted, and the vibration of the planet is raised. and activated through meditation, which is the primary work.

More on the "Ground Crew Away Team": Their galactic mission is to BE "First Contact" out in the world, by attracting others on a 5D frequency, and especially by connecting with new recognizable fellow ground crewmates. Having these divine encounters *under the radar*, they share the encouraging message that Humans are OurSelves Our own means to Freedom. These "contactees" may then in turn, inform and inspire others with the message that Humans are now connecting for the purpose of standing forth as the real and rightful heirs of the planet Earth.

As the message is shared exponentially, there is a quotient that is reached. This is known as the "divine proportion", or "golden ratio". (The exact number is unknown, but is a percentage of the Human population required for planetary ascension). Once this quotient is reached, Humanity as a whole, in their Self-declared Freedom, only then are to be assisted. Benevolent E.T.s are standing by to help usher Our species across the dimensional threshold. Therefore it is imperative that Our numbers increase to assure Our liberation, and Our exit all the way out through the frequency grid of the programmed matrix.

The Soul-ution is brought forth, not by merely averting imposed chaos or even by counterbalancing it, and certainly not by resisting it, but by *transcending* the extreme polarization of it. By sharing the transcendent message to "hold the 5D current" – at the appropriate time, an interdependent viable portion of the population stands forth and profoundly REVEALS itself apart from Fear….. and the next paradigm materializes.

…..

The Ground Crew in general, are the founding parents of a Self-determined, Self-empowered New Paradigm of Oneness, in diversity.

Anchoring-in the 5th dimensional frequency is accomplished by:

*intentionally interlinking with one another energetically,
*breaking free of 3D programming of extreme polarization and the self-serving hierarchy that perpetuates it,
*proactively embodying and promoting wholeness within Our species,
*establishing a New energetic Paradigm through practicing the art of Allowance with Balance (See chapter 13),
*holding the 5D current in the event of any and all evolutionary chaos….. and beyond.

In so doing, the old hierarchical victim/victimizer consciousness is transcended, and the New Paradigm emerges. Big congratulations to Humanity and the entire team will be in order!! **Continued holding of the current by these "pre-launch parents" will be required for the sustaining and nurturing of the viable New Paradigm through its infancy.** Until then, joy in the journey is the mainstay.

Through small groups, these C of C 5D energy nodes are pioneering the basic template for the inauguration of Self-governance for thriving in Our new planetary community.

CHAPTER 8
Why Groups?
What do Groups Have to do with Self-governance?

We are individuals - individuated Soul beings, make no mistake about it. So what's the big deal about groups in relation to Self-governance, with so many metaphysical advisors today pointing to *self this* and *self that?* There is self-care, self-healing, self-determination, self-serve, self-realization, self-sustaining, self-fulfillment, DIY (do it your-self), self-love, self-discovery, creating your *own* reality, and individual sovereignty. Wouldn't all this focus on "self", make group gatherings as a means to evolution, passé? And what if I'm just not a "joiner"?

There are supremely knowledgeable individuals who can brilliantly espouse and teach New Paradigm consciousness on a solo stage, or be a captivating leader in a metaphysical workshop. The real evidence for being a New Paradigm emissary, however, is in how vibrationally cooperative, intuitive, and balancing one is….. when creating as a participant…..in a group.

"Independent thinking alone is not suited to interdependent reality. Independent people who do not have the maturity to think and act interdependently may be good individual producers, but they won't be good leaders or team players. They're not coming from the paradigm of inter-dependence necessary to succeed in marriage, family or organizational reality." Stephen Covey, *7 Habits of Highly Effective People*, 1989

> The familiar and much coveted 3D "IN*dependence*" operates on a different frequency shall we say, than 5D "INTER*dependence*".

The capability to integrate effectively and authentically as one's true Self, within a group frequency of 5D Oneness, is what upholds and embues the qualities inherent to a New Paradigm community. This vibration translates on a global scale and can be called **Earth kinship. As such, it can neither be legislated, assigned, granted, nor bestowed, and isn't anything you "join". Earth kinship is awakened from within.**

Cs of C ARE WHERE WE PRACTICE EARTH KINSHIP. *As in "the <u>meek</u> that shall INHERIT the earth."* This is the revelation of true equality and kinship. It is experienced amongst those who are aware that HUMANS, AS A WHOLE, ARE THE RIGHTFUL HEIRS OF EARTH, without need of oversight.

What is meekness? Here is an acrostic of M E E K:
M y E mbodiment   (of)   E arth K inship

5D MEEKNESS IS THE NEW BOLDNESS !
The "movers and shakers, and rock stars of 5D"
are those who are meek.
This can be as intoxicating and adventurous
for yourSelf as you allow it to be!

New Paradigm Meekness is, are you ready for this? Self-loving, Self-responsible, inter-dependent sovereignty, and proactive, healthy cooperation, for the highest, best good of All. It's definitely a new status and a new way of being!

What many individuals are on guard against in terms of Oneness - *and understandably so!* - is "assimilation into the herd" and the danger of losing the individuated self. **Earth kinship, as is discovered and practiced in Cs of C, is never to be confused with lumping Humans together into an indistinct, muted, mushy, lowest common denominator intellect.** That kind of 3D mind control (along with the associated judgement and resistance) is actually what We have RIGHT NOW, inside the programmed fear matrix!

The New Paradigm is based not on 3D conformity that We know as "hive mind", "group-think", "collectivist soup", "status quo", "mindless consensus" or "apathy", but on quite the contrary. Earth kinship of the New Paradigm is based on each one's fully Self-expressed uniqueness, as a distinguished marvel, and respected within the myriad of diverse facets that make up the One whole.

Conscious chAMbering groups are microcosms of planetary-wide kinship. The allowing/balancing Presence, and love you have for yourSelf demonstrated in a group, is who you are in 5D. Again, it's nothing one "joins", it's Self-activated DNA Presence. We're approaching this great Shift of the Ages with the attitude that either We're All ascending, or none of Us are ascending. There's no more good guy/bad guy, there's just Us Earth kin! It's not Our call as to whether anyone would or should get "left behind". In this plane of awareness, We are here to simply awaken and learn Self-empowerment..... in Oneness.

A C of C is where We get to practice interfacing as Earth kin, and it's an understatement that We certainly do need practice! How Our 5D Presence vibrates in a group, is how Our Presence vibrates in the world at large. How We embody Earth kinship is critical to Our galactic mission, in regard to creating Humanity's future, as informed and enlightened beings.

In cooperation with my Earth kin, I can embrace a group-Soul consciousness in a C of C. It is an opportunity for me to practice and learn how to:
..... Listen. Be Present.
..... Be responsible for maintaining the vibrational frequency and the energetic flow.
..... Recognize and embody 5D qualities.
..... Let go of old patterns that are better left in 3D.
..... Discern. Be in a galactic context.

….. Let go of bossiness and tendencies for the need to control and dominate.

….. Identify and let go of what might cause me to shrink back and withhold mySelf energetically.

….. Work and play well with others based in the art of Allowance and Balance, bookends of co-creation.

….. Facilitate proceedings proactively without defaulting to the 3D co-dependent leader/follower model.

….. Love mySelf in a group. Set firm personal boundaries from a place of Self-love, not defensiveness or resistance.

….. Self-regulate.

….. Co-create without defaulting to 3D compromise or acquiescing.

….. Get a higher perspective on "drama". Appreciate diversity. Respect choices even when I disagree.

….. Challenge mySelf and take some risks. Alchemize.

….. Validate All players in All their various roles, letting go of judgementalism and divisive labels.

….. Take 100% responsibility for my own experience.

….. Find my unique voice and vibrate as to my passion and commitments.

….. Have a sense of humor in joyful communication.

…..Give, serve, and receive, exponentially in community.

….. Combine Self-determination and Self-responsibility with inter-dependence and vibrate as One Soul.

….. Choose the Soul-aligned 5D organic reality over the transhumanist counterfeit.

….. Develop new 5D consciousness empowering abilities.

…..Share this vibrational frequency out in the world which authenticates increased 5D capacity.

….. Let in possibility itself, organically augmenting the group's energy. Trust the Process.

"To *know* oneself is to study oneself
in action with another person."
Bruce Lee

CHAPTER 9
Let's Go Deeper In

The work of Cs of C is accomplished in "radical inclusivity", not in tightening the screws of control, with the "creative light" mounting resistance against the "unscrupulous dark". Nor is it through raising objections back and forth ad infinitum. Oneness flows from a consciousness that aligns with a 5D template of sacred geometry, of light, sound, frequency, and vibration.

"WE ARE ONE"
DOES NOT MEAN WE ARE ALL THE SAME,
OR THAT THERE ARE NO MORE PERSONAL
BOUNDARIES OR PREFERENCES,
OR THAT WE SIMPLY COME UNDER YET ANOTHER
IMPOSED HIERARCHY (TOUTED TO BE "GOOD").

ONENESS IS ALL PARTS THRIVING TOGETHER AS ONE BODY, much the same as our physical biological body does, with all of its various parts and functions, making up the one whole. The next paradigm calls Us OUT of sameness, and the way We have been viewed in the past by Our custodians as herds of swine. Oneness invites Us into who We say that We really are. We are here to learn the ways of love, as the New Human archetype. Fear of leaving the "barnyard" and "stockyards", is an old paradigm 3D-drenched program. Just recognize it as such and renew your mind. **We do not conquer the darkness, We come out of division.**

Moving out of the paradigm of fear and control and into "We are One", will mean that We each distinctively have free will to Self-determine personal boundaries and preferences. It may seem daunting, impractical, or utterly impossible to interlink within a radically inclusive group Presence, that is at once, very compassionate *and* powerfully Self-rebalancing. The reason for having any of these reservations to let go of the familiar, is that because of the simulated reality, **We have never seen *real Freedom* before, for a people**. We tend to fear the unknown, so reticence is understandable. But it just so happens that inter-linking, underscored with Self-love and respect for All scentient beingness, is **the litmus for being 5D galactically-identifiable**.

This reinforced, affirming Freedom that vibrates in a C of C, reads as a viable heartbeat of 5D Presence on the galactic fetal monitor as it were. It is this 5D Presence that is a sign of life, detectable to those upper dimensionals who have a vested interest in assisting Humanity at this time of graduation/birthing. Our liberation necessitates assistance from an upper level, but before that can be offered, **We Humans must evolve on Our own.**

Starting with OurSelves, the work of chAMbering is that of opening Our heart (4D) in non-judgemental, unconditional, forgiving love, and then assisting others in their liberation and transcendence **from 3D, through 4D, into 5D**. A C of C is the ⁖ chrysalis ⁖ of Our species' life experience.

Through the opening of
The 4th Dimensional ⁖ Portal of *the heart*…..
3D Consciousness translates to 5D Consciousness:
3D………. ⁖ ……….5D

3D		5D
depressing victimstance…	⁖	…healthy & proactive sovereignty;
judgement & fear…	⁖	…discernment & transcendence;
uninformed ignorance…	⁖	…spiritual intelligence;
co-dependent dysfunction…	⁖	…Self-responsibility & wisdom;
scarcity…	⁖	…abundance;
hierarchy/control…	⁖	… interdependent leadership;
ego posturing/competing…	⁖	…co-creation/healthy cooperation;
Humans mined as resources…	⁖	… Self-empowerment as rightful heirs;
illusion/separation/strife/trickery…	⁖	…peace/All is One/allowance/balance;
counterfeit to divine plan…	⁖	…claiming/retaining Our Soul.

The group consciousness which carries the energy signature of these Soul-level qualities, is heart-centered 5th dimensional Presence. Releasing the old patterns of 3D separation consciousness is required for emerging through the 4D awakened heart and bridging to 5D New Human. **Leaving the familiar 3D "fishbowl" containment and becoming the new 5D species that animates on the "dry land" of Freedom, is a leap in consciousness!** Each must do more than talk about it ! Each 5D candidate "goldfish", having opened their heart, must choose for themSelves to then make the leap out of the fishbowl.

ChAMbers of consciousness serve as the pre-launch and proving ground for Self-governed planetary community and as such, raise the frequency of the entire planet and All inhabitants. The old subjugation and control will be obsolete, upon graduation or launch into the new paradigm. Participants in Cs of C are holding the vision and broadcasting the frequency of Oneness to include All – both light and dark, *as well as those who are still asleep* under the old paradigm control programming. So with the grounding of the divine proportion, along with galactic assistance, the entire Human species may then be triggered awake, having the opportunity to make the leap into fully Human and Self-activate their DNA.

> "Where 3 or more are gathered as One, in I AM Presence,
> there are upper dimensional and etheric helpers,
> assisting in the REVEALING of
> the true luminescence
> of Our Soul."

Honoring and mastering the lower dimension (3rd) for ascending into the not "better", but "higher" (5th) is Our journey inward/homeward. It is an upward spiral of Self-love.

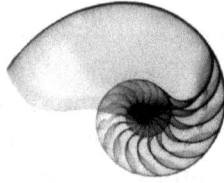

PART 3
EMBRACING
TRANSCENDENCE

CHAPTER 10
ChAMbering.....
On the Self-love Path to Mastery

The Self-love path to mastery is truly a leap in consciousness.

At this stage of awareness, Self-love
can be appropriated in two different ways:
"self-love, in-service-to-self"-or- "Self-love, in-service-to-others".
Love your neighbor as your~"self"
(lower case "s" service-to-self)
-or-
Love your neighbor as your~"Self"
(upper case "S" service-to-others)

"Service-to-self" *self-love,* is based on separation from, and misalignment with, Source. Dark workers actually ARE in service to others –inadvertently– by motivating the light to evolve. And they DO serve others, but only as it benefits *their own self* in some way, usually more directly than indirectly.

"Service-to-others" *Self-love,* is based on trust and alignment with, Source. Light workers serve both the light and the dark intentionally, by embodying and experiencing Oneness for the highest, best good of All.

In 5D, this service "to-self /to-others" distinction
is a more subtle contrast than in
the extreme polarization of good and evil
that 3D typically characterizes.
5D "service-to-self" and 5D "service-to-others" people
are not as easily distinguished as one might think,
as they can actually both be quite effective as New Paradigmers.
Viewed in the bigger picture, and with discernment,
these two appropriations are in play as *divine complements.*

In a C of C, there will be dark/light complements that are in "service to-self/to-others" that attract and combine for the purpose of learning how Oneness works *realistically*. It is paramount that Oneness translates out of the limitations of 3D *concepts,* into the New Paradigm 5D *experience.* As long as the set intention is to evolve together, these complementary expressions can cause a leap in alchemical harmonizing, and up-leveling of discernment. This can be the case as long as the energetic vortex is set firmly, prior to or at the onset of the gathering, with authority. By establishing a space of Mahatma Divine Love, no vibration lower than this is allowed.

The idea for vitalizing real Freedom through chAMbering is this: Maintain love for yourSelf, and have respect for All scentient beings' right to exist. Show up in an experiential meeting with your metaphysical peers - who may or may not agree on all things, but who probably agree on some or many things. When you can choose to co-create with those with whom you may disagree on some or many things, while maintaining Self-love, then there is hope for maintaining love and respect vibrationally out in the world. 4D is the heart portal for either Self-love or self-love, and is intrinsic to 5D experience.

AGAIN, it is important to note that no one is asked to *condone* the free will choices made by others!! What is to be inherently respected is the *choice* to *exercise free will* for making their choices. A chAMber is where We get to experience the nature and potential of Our grownup Soul-Selves, for practicing respect for free will in general. This is even as it refracts through the prism of Our Human diversity, that could easily be described as untamed and consistently wacky! The Oneness frequency replaces 3D pyramidal control. The 5D Oneness frequency rests upon free will that Self-regulates and brings no harm. Do not let 3D skepticism block your ability to imagine real Freedom, possibly for the first time, beyond the control grid and extreme polarity. …..I strongly encourage Us to keep imagining what real Freedom must feel like.

Cs of C thus serve as basic training for future Human inter-galactic affiliations and summits. Softening the banners of the harsh distinctions within 3D into a 5D emphasis is a simple idea, but certainly not easy! **Because of the little matter of people wanting to be "right"**, Oneness tends to get displaced handily, thus duality perpetuates. In that case nothing changes – and Humanity doesn't evolve naturally on schedule, Our Soul essence gets seized by off-planet interests, and light in the galaxy doesn't increase. We've definitely got some fine-tuning to do, and fast!

Peaceful cooperation that is Self-determined, non-hierarchical, and Self-governing, is the vibrational evidence for a New Paradigm that is **OF, BY, and FOR Earth inhabitants**. Experimenting with the potential of Self-love expressed on this 5D frequency, is what draws positive galactic attention. *Our galactic supporters are waiting for a proportion of Us to mature as a coherent species* before they'll step in to lend a hand. How that will manifest remains to be seen, but this much is sure - **We cannot do this planetary 3D-to-5D transition purely on Our own. Garnering galactic assistance is imperative for this evolutionary shift, and Cs of C as the 5D societal precursors, are galactic receptors and transmitters.** Validating the Self with love, and regard for the One Soul-Self, is the portal opener to becoming One planetary people.

"Love your neighbor as yourSelf." - Jesus the Christ
(Not ~ as if ~ they were you, they ARE you. Love them accordingly.)

"Namaste" - (I bow to the divine in you.) - Sanskrit greeting

"In Lak'ech Ala K'in"- (I am another yourSelf.
I am you and you are me.) - Ancient Mayan greeting

"Without darkness, one cannot know light." - Author unknown

"Your task is not to seek for love, but merely to seek and find all the barriers within yourself that you have built against it." - Rumi

CHAPTER 11
A "Coup of Consciousness"
Through Soul-Awareness

The Human species is on a collision course with the complete absorption into the soulless machinery that supports the simulated reality. Our evolution hinges on finding a solution to this archonically-inspired absorption. This solution is one which *has not ever been seen before* – one which is awakened from within, that is then brought forth practically:

a SOUL-ution.

The Soul-ution is: Showing up as a new evolutionary Presence on Earth, in the claiming and retaining of Our Souls, the seat of Our existence. It is in cooperation with one another that We discover the organic, divine blueprint for the claiming of Humanity's birthright, and Our planetary inheritance. That "sounds" good, but how will the claiming and retaining of Our Souls ever happen, when the artificial constraints that separate Us All, are being levied so heavily against Us?

**In a C of C there is new portal-opening energy
that shifts the game
from enslaved life as We've known it,
to the game of liberation:**

**the playing field: RADICAL INCLUSIVITY,
the procedural frequency: RESPECT FOR ALL,
how to advance: SELF-RESPONSIBILITY/LOVE,
the object/galactic mission: BIRTHING A 5D PARADIGM.**

This is the game being played when either of the 2 formats of Cs of C are activated, in an "ongoing community", or in an "away team".

**In a newfound energy field of Oneness,
a GROUP-SOUL can come forth,
ushering-in a new Human Presence,
that establishes 5D stewardship for Earth.**

Those who generate a group-Soul, coalesce on a material plane that finds its basis in the higher realm of the Soul. **A group-Soul does not displace or supersede the worth of an individuated Soul, but underscores it**. By catalyzing and assisting the participating individual Souls that make up the group-Soul, each one's unique purpose is more elegantly embodied and accentuated.

A group-Soul is different from having "a kindred spirit". Much more than having similar interests and attitudes within a 3D *organ-ization*, a group-Soul exists as a 5D multi-dimensional life form or *organ-ism*. Each individual Soul has access to the energy radiating from their group-Soul that augments and amplifies their own radiance. The existence of a group-Soul births exceptionally new 5D possibilities!

A C of C is composed of at least 3 individual like-frequencied Humans. By definition, the word "group" is an aggregate of several units, (3 at the least). A *group of people* requires a different level of cooperation than does a couple or duo. This Soul-aware organism that is comprised of at least 3 individual Humans, maintains no formal membership, and has a "permeable membrane" (as afforded by free will).

Its vibrational frequency of Oneness is foundationally of a trinarian quality (three aspects, mind/spirit/body, operating as One) and promotes planetary peace and wholeness. The more people there are in one chAMber does not make it better. In fact, with upwards to 15...18...21... in a group-Soul C of C meeting, there can be loss of felt intimacy, unless participants are already very vibrationally bonded, in which case the number is inconsequential.

Choosing to evolve naturally from the 3rd to 5th dimension of consciousness, is holding the energetic space of possibility **for the highest, best good of ALL**. Anything less than inclusive of ALL is separation from the whole, which would belong with the denser 3rd dimension. The fact that the chAMbering of 5D consciousness is now present on Earth, is an indication that a dimensional shift into Soul-awareness, an exciting and profound coup of higher consciousness..... is occurring!

A new baseline and frame of reference is imminent, not just for those who are awake, but for ALL Earth people. The **"highest best good of All concerned" is far from the syrupy sentimental, corruptible 3D thought construct of what has been called "the common or greater good".** Highest best good of All includes *every individual's* highest and best good, as well as that of the planet's. On behalf of the highest and best good of All, Cs of C are assemblage points that impact the composite consciousness by setting the new precedent as that of a Self-governed planetary 5D community.

Deep within each Human being is a desire to Self-discover the creator Soul that We are. Through the mode of the heart, a C of C's alchemy is quickened, sculpted, and supported by Universal Law (described more fully in Chapter 13). These group-Soul inner workings have the ability to not only affect, but to alchemically materialize reality. When aligned with Source, a chAMbering group-Soul is capable of broadcasting a frequency that corresponds to the geometry of the etheric vibrational pattern of that which is desired for manifestation - in this case, a New Paradigm of peace and Freedom.

The following chapter describes an energy in which the participants are engrossed for the purpose of working deceitfully in the world. This heavy-duty complement to Cs of C is in antithesis to the Soul-ution.

CHAPTER 12
"Parlors" of Consciousness

Dark siders certainly do make things "interesting".

The energy of a group's consciousness can be harnessed by those who are wielding the control. This is done when dark workers use group energy to **reserve** *what would be considered to be the highest and best good,* in manifesting it ONLY for themselves. This more narrow appropriation of energy *imitates* a chAMber of consciousness, except that supreme service-to-self is the motivation.

For this dark counterpart to chAMbering, I have coined the word *"parloring"*. This is alchemical manipulation that is conducted within what I'll call a "Parlor" of Consciousness.

The word "parlor" is largely an antiquated concept today. In the past, it was a lovely, inviting room where guests were formally entertained. Parlors were for formal albeit comfortable, restful sitting and lounging, and conversing, and where delightful music could be offered, and elegant refreshments might be served. This brings to mind an air of the aristocracy, the genteel class, or intelligentsia – the socially exclusionary and materially elite. A consciousness *"parlor"*(an extraction of "polar" in combo with "parlay", translating to *successful exploitation*) is the manipulating and directing of a group's energetic consciousness, with the intention to subjugate others outside the group, according to self-serving will.

The purpose of *"parloring"* is the exercise of ascendancy and superiority over others, in order to benefit the controllers' own deliberate, willful, self-serving ends, with no concern for any detrimental fallout for others. Let the reader know that dark rituals twist and painfully contort innocence and natural life as a part of these sinister *parlors*, in order to maintain their abusive hierarchy. There are many books, materials, and documentaries which expose the conspiratorial realm of deception and pyramid of control that runs planet Earth. This is the cruelty of black magick and it is how Our species has been ruled, from the beginning.

It is not the purpose of this book to focus on the contrast between *"ChAMbers"* and *"Parlors" of consciousness*, other than to open up the bigger picture. The main focus is magnifying beauty through *ChAMbers of Consciousness,* by increasing the bandwidth and potency of such. To do so, it is of necessity that the existence of these *Parlors,* be acknowledged.

Consciousness Parlors are galactic and terrestrial realities and are [at best], 4D complements to Cs of C. Both *chAMbers* and *parlors* avail themselves to galactic assistance through light and dark alliances respectively. Beyond this chapter, for a deeper depiction of these *parlors* AND their chAMber complement, I invite you to read my fictional novel *Soul Shade.*

The black magickian overlords see Humans as nothing more than their resource commodity. They will not allow Human energy to just slip out from their control simply because Humans are poised to naturally evolve. Neither will they relax the control grid upholding the matrix "simulation/illusion", the medium in which their "Human resource" is cultivated. They will not just relinquish their control over planet Earth, simply on account of natural evolution - quite the contrary.

The dark controllers have factored in the calculated risk of the natural evolvement of their engineered Human slave species, and they have developed effective ways of retarding Our maturation. **This interference to Our growth can be expected to be applied full strength, prior to Humans remembering and finding their connection to their Soul.** The virginal essence of the Human Soul as a commodity, is what is planned on being "harvested", just as any growing plant crop would be.

For the distinction between "chAMbers" and "parlors" of consciousness, to draw an example from Nature, there is a categorical difference between the terms "chrysalis" and "cocoon". Although similar, they are not exactly the same and many people who do not realize this, use the terms interchangeably, which is inaccurate. A chrysalis is the correct term for the casing that a caterpillar emerges from, through metamorphosis, as a butterfly (known for its beauty in Creation). A cocoon is the correct term for the casing that a caterpillar emerges from, through metamorphosis, as a moth (known to be more destructive). So you might say that a consciousness chAMber (the light) is to a butterfly's chrysalis, as a consciousness "parlor" (the dark) is to a moth's cocoon. The basic concept for how these crucibles of consciousness produce results are similar through the power of intention. It is the orientation of service-to-"others" or service-to-"self" that is the major distinction.

Parloring is hierarchical group-weaving of will by Humans devoid of compassion or empathy. In service-to-self at the expense of others, as subjugators of Earth, for self-advancement, *parlors* are out of alignment with Source. A *Parlor of Consciousness* is the space in which dark conspiracies are conceived and maintained. The idea here is not to recoil in fear and/or judgement from this reality, but to simply observe

Humanity in the wholeness of "Our" evolution, with light and dark playing their integral roles, in the metamorphosis of Our *entire* species. We are evolving from 3D larvae (caterpillar), to 4D pupa (transition), to 5D adult (butterfly).

Inherent within the word "Source" is *OUR*; S*OUR*CE. *Parloring* groups disacknowledge the S-OUR-CE of Our being. They are a distortion of *chAMbering* groups, which are authentic group consciousness that naturally and creatively acknowledge the S-OUR-CE of Our being. Parlor-ers acquire energy by power brokering, in hierarchical separation and superiority that is out of alignment with the S-OUR-CE of their being.

Parlor-ers are in league with artificial and contrived machinations which support the parasitic appetites of archonically-driven, dark galactic forces. The energy sustenance of these parasites is what some call "loosch" (my spelling), and comes from the traumatized emotions of Humanity. "Loosch" is generated and perpetuated by means of imposed heinous crimes of pain, trauma, and torture, to the detriment of the sense world of the uninformed Human masses.

It is a bit shocking, but from a higher perspective on Humans evolving in a free will Universe, both types of transformational assemblies, *ChAMbers and Parlors* are working on behalf of Our metamorphosis. Both are in 4D Self-love/self-love heart space, just on differently aligned paths, light and dark. On planet Earth prior to graduation, **contrary to popular belief, workers of light and dark undertakings alike, are eligible for emerging from 3rd, through the 4th, and into the 5th dimension, the dawn of a New Paradigm.**

Continuing on with the Nature theme as Our teacher in the next section, We can learn more about how Humans have been imprinted by *parloring*, and the group-weaving of will from the arachnid template.

ChAMbers of Consciousness
THE CONSUMMATE WEB BUILDERS:
Spiders

"Come into My Parlor, Said the Spider to the Fly….."
Mary Howitt, 1829

Is there a connection between "spider energy" and the "world wide web" ?,,,,, well, what do *you* think? How about "web crawlers", "spider bots", "spider search engines", and "spider drones", hmmmm? This is a theme We need to be aware of!

How this works is pretty easy. The victimizers, or spiders if you will, construct an energetic web for ensnarement. Then taking the energy from the web-entangled victims, their "flies", they parlay or *parlor* that energy to their own immediate and long term advantage. This is to the extreme detriment of overall well-being of the "flies". There is no judgement by this writer, of the natural 3D world as it exists in its raw reality with spiders, webs – their inherent trickery, subterfuge, and all. It's all here to provide Us with an unmistakable picture that points to the threshold, the crossing over of which, will be the next leap in Human evolution.

There are plenty of 3D conditioning and uncloaked spider messages in Our frame of reference:

Little Miss Muffet, by Mother Goose
"Little Miss Muffet, sat on a tuffet,
Eating her curds and whey.
*Along came a **spider**,*
And sat down beside her,
And frightened Miss Muffet away."

…..We're afraid of spiders alright! Like Miss Muffet, Humans have historically said to their enslavers, "Here – take my resources, I'll do what you say, just leave me alone….. and please don't hurt me!"

The motto of Bohemian Grove is *"Weaving **Spiders** Come Not Here."* (Bohemian Grove is an elitist summer camp for globalist leaders, located in the CA Redwood forest.) This motto is a line from Shakespeare's *A Midsummer Night's Dream* Act 2, Scene 2 …..I.e. Bohemian Grove is not a place for working, but for recreation. It's a place for globalist "spiders" to just rest and play, chilling out together.

The Eensy Weensy **Spider** -camp song-
"Eensy Weensy Spider sat on a water spout.
Down came the rain and washed the spider out.
Out came the sun and dried up all the rain,
And the eensy weensy spider crawled up the spout again."
…..Spiders are hardy and determined and relentless – Like a horror movie quote "I'm baaaaack!"

Spiders in general are associated with fear. Halloween brings out huge, black, hairy spider decorations to scare Us.

In the sci fi futuristic film "Minority Report" [2002, director Steven Spielberg] there was a disturbing scene where cold technological **spider drones** were sent to track down the Human protagonist and thankfully did not detect him underwater. *Phew!*

Spider webs or cobwebs, are the stereotypic embellishment to any creepy, terrifying haunted house. Cobwebs are old dusty spider webs, reminding Us that ensnaring control methods in the halls of darkness have been there a long time, and are quite enmeshed and ancient. Humans do not generally welcome cobwebs in their homes, but clear this residue out of the corners, especially for Spring cleaning or when company is expected!

UN-SPIDER.org is an official UN program. United Nations Space-Based Platform for Information for Disaster Management and Emergency Response.

Interesting Facts About Spiders:
*Spiders spin their silken webs, reminiscent of how the controlled media "spins" fallacious coherence within a projected illusion.
*Spiders can masquerade as insects by pretending that two of their 8 legs are antennae, so as to appear to be an insect. The other 6-legged insects are fooled into thinking the spider is another insect, and go to their demise. Remind you of anyone? Politicians maybe?
*Spiders do not eat their prey, they first liquefy it by their venom, and then they suck the liquid. This goes on in the dark halls.
* Humans have a natural aversion to spiders. Fear of spiders, or Arachnophobia, is one of the most common specific phobias.

Parlors of Consciousness, as they've operated through the Ages in 3D, WILL become obsolete, as the parasitic nature of the dark galactic stakeholders becomes identified from within Our burgeoning 5D sovereign perspective. **In the coming years or days, many controllers will find themselves, as spiders, being blown from their webs of deceit, as dark and light paths integrate in order to evolve….. in healthy alignment with the higher, divine plan.**

We must evolve in order to put a halt to Humanity's enslavement. By graduating 3D and moving into 5D, archonically-inspired contracts are revoked, and all previous offers are terminated by "Us", the REVEALED, rightful, sovereign heirs to planet Earth.

Cs of C manifest New Paradigm reality through the *interweaving of hearts, not self-will.* They radiate and activate Oneness on behalf of All. **So how do we bring refreshment and clear out all of the planetary spider and cob webs from the four corners of Our world? Discovering Our power through the 4 Universal Laws, is CRUCIAL, and a C of C accelerates the process.**

CHAPTER 13
The 4 Primary Universal Laws -
Tenets of Our Next Paradigm of Peace

The real question is, are We, as a species, finished and complete with this era of hostility and separation? No? Yes? Applying the Universal Laws in a C of C raises the bar for facing Our fear of: Equanimity within the diversity of Oneness, practicalities around ascension from 3D into 5D reality, and being the ones to REVEAL the new Human archetype NOW.

"…..upon the wisdom of these Universal Laws will rest the future. They are the foundation of the new paradigm of existence."
Becoming pg 92;
Bridger House Publishers

THE 4 PRIMARY UNIVERSAL LAWS ARE THE ONLY LAWS NEEDED FOR 5TH DIMENSIONAL INTERFACE.

* All of the Earth plane players, dark and light, have access to Laws 1 & 2 – regardless of their spiritual/political/vibrational alignment.
   1. The Universal Law of Attraction:
 Like attracts like; opposites also attract as it benefits to clarify what you are attracting.
   2. The Universal Law of Creative Intent:
Implementation of one's desire to create a particular experience or manifestation through appropriating through will and deliberate thought. This is where the motivation for dark and light, service-to-self/service-to-others is distinguished.

NOW HERE'S THE *REALLY* GOOD NEWS!
* Only those who are aligned to the highest and best good of All, have access to Laws 3 & 4, which provides a distinct advantage for those who are here to transcend that which is mimicry of the

Light with its inherent deception.
3. The Universal Law of Allowance:
Love in action in the context of free will and Self-responsibility, transcending the need to egoically control people or situations.
4. The Universal Law of Balance:
In concert with the first 3 Laws, instability, dissonance, and tension are addressed by harmonizing and bringing resolution, while strongly upholding Self-love and the integrity of the New Paradigm.

These Universal Laws are on tap to overtake old paradigm man-made laws. Embodying these as Trinarians (graduates out of the limitations of the false binarian reality) is key to encompassing and dissolving the enslaving agenda.

The 3D self wants to know," What are the RULES for these chAMber meetings??   How is this supposed to work, and who's in charge?" …..There are no "rules" or a dogmatic belief system for a C of C, other than trusting yourSelf and those present, to express themSelves with respect for All, along with some gentle, agreed-upon guidelines, all grounded in the 4 basic Universal Laws.

More on the Universal Law of Allowance…..
Discovering the distinctions between "tolerance", "patience", and "allowance", in the context of co-creation, is largely the experience that is available in a C of C. These 3 graduated refinements of Allowance are similar, but not interchangeable.
"3D Tolerance", fairly common in 3D (along with intolerance!), is practiced while retaining the estimation that there is something wrong or unpleasant, but under the circumstances, teeth are gritted and the situation is endured until that time when hopefully the pressure lifts or something gets changed.
"4D Patience" is found particularly amongst people who are kind-hearted and compassionate in 4D reality. Patience is extended when there is something occurring that is interpreted as imperfect and needs to improve and advance, hopefully sooner than later.

"5D Allowance" operates at a 5D altitude and frequency that vibrationally neutralizes any feelings of lower vibrational judgemental emotion that makes anyone or anything, in essence, "wrong" or "bad". While non-judgement of the essence of a thing is key, one may still choose their own personal preferences. Allowance is proactive and is not to be confused with being passive, abused, martyred, or being a pathetic "doormat". Allowing is having a non-judgemental, transcendent way of being. The 3rd Universal Law of Allowing is a remarkably effective 5D navigational ability, especially when experienced in correlation with the 4th Universal Law of bringing "Balance".

More on the Universal Law of Balance…..
The equilibrium in 5D brought about by Balance, is not forced or heavy-handed as in 3D. Vibrational Balance is not *3D authoritarian*, but *5D authoritative energy*. Balance is Self-determined, and is a graduation from the ignorance of 1.) who one really is, and 2.) the manufactured imbalance of the left/right survival game of victimizer/victim. Balance does not mean being devoid of any contrast, as in "boring" or "bland. Bringing the creative Balance is as exciting as surfing! With it comes refreshment, in regard to Self-responsibility for maintaining boundaries. Balance is brought in the interest of the highest best good of ALL, and is especially artful when experienced in correlation with the Universal Law of "Allowing".

In 5D, Allowance and Balance go creatively hand in hand. Allowance alone, without Balance, is a sappy 3D cop out. Balance alone, without Allowance, is egoic 3D control. Allowance and Balance in partnership, is a transcendent means to Self-empowerment, ending the distortions of architected chaos. Using these two Laws in tandem restores the natural order to not only any gathering where you show up as 5D, but also to Our planet.

ChAMbers of Consciousness
SELF-REGULATING
THROUGH ALLOWANCE AND BALANCE

Self-regulating is mandated in productive chAMbering. As Cs of C are the precursor for thriving as a Self-governed people in the next paradigm, the imperative of Self-regulating is stressed in this chapter!!

So who and what is this "Self"….. doing the regulating?
After two-plus centuries of earnest effort by Freedom lovers, to apply what was professed so boldly in *The Declaration of Independence*, We are only just now making a collective realization as to what it is, that supposedly was so "self-evident".

"We hold these truths to be **self-evident**,
that all Men are created equal, that
they are endowed by their Creator
with certain unalienable Rights,
that among these are Life, Liberty, and the Pursuit of Happiness.
[I also believe that We have a right to know who Our progenitors are,
but that's a digression.]

The realization We're making now, is about the "estate" of the "self". We now know that the famed "self-evident" utterance was prophetic. *That 1776* "self" was serving as the placeholder for the latent 21st century, multi-dimensional, timeless "Self". Self that would be capable of evincing these truths so plainly, is illuminated when We apply the distinctions in *ascension language*. Lowercase *"s"self* is 3D egoic self, distinguished from uppercase *"S"* Self that is 5D Soul-aware Self with Self-activated DNA.

Created as being equal - with All other "selves/Selves", is now coming into view in terms of Oneness. In order to apprehend what *the Declaration* meant by "self-evident", one must simply exceed the limited capacity of 3D consciousness. On this side of ascension, Our Soul-illumined "Selves" have been hiding….. in plain sight!!!!!

Now that We can observe current life alongside the thread of Human history, We have a higher and much more informed, perspective. As a result, We can each actually choose to take our very own place in a Humanity that is One indivisible, majestic whole. Today We can relate with a 5D "Self", having the capacity to embody Self-evincing truths as <u>endowed</u> (not merely bestowed) by Our Creator.

This new plane of awareness has opened the bigger picture for hailing the composite planetary consciousness on a new frequency. Besides exposing the tyrannical and dark control mechanisms that have ruled over Us since the beginning, the new archetypal 5D "Self" is being *REVEALED* through **the vibration of Allowance with Balance. This "Self" is the basis of Self-regulating.**

"3D self-regulating" has mostly been deciding whether to conform or not, and whether or not to violate the enforced rules that utilize fear and incur punishment. That dispensation now serves as an onramp for Humans to transpose this control paradigm to a higher energy range that incorporates Self-governance. This level of 5D Self-responsibility is at once inside of, and transcendent to, the 3D matrix.

3D fear-based egoic control mechanisms that were designed to attempt to protect and keep order in Our Human affairs proceedings can now be retired, such as: Parliamentary procedure, Robert's Rules of Order, a sergeant-at-arms, a talking stick, dogmatic enforcement of sacred text fundamentalism, a timer, a bailiff, or an appointed/elected strong presiding chieftain.

Everyone in the chAMbering group is responsible to Self-regulate. This is accomplished when each one's facilitation is offered in respect and consideration, based in the understanding that **Our inheritance is indivisible**, and that We are co-creating experientially as One. The next chapter is a simple step by step outline of how to conduct a Self-governed meeting, start to finish.

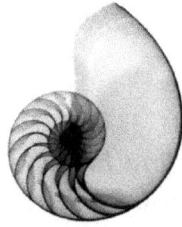

PART 4
FACILITATION!

22 PRACTICAL STEPS FOR
INITIATING and FACILITATING
YOUR CHAMBER OF CONSCIOUSNESS

QUICK START ESSENTIALS
for becoming adept at
initiating and participating
in 5D transformative gatherings.

! If you're already part of a 4D-to-5D community that could
perhaps be even more Soul-aware and affective, then
please consider gifting them with
a copy of this book or at least a photocopy of these practical steps.

It only takes 3 to form a chAMber of consciousness. The
following step-by-step guideline is for anyone and everyone who
would like to be a part of the transformation of Our society and
healthy immune system for Our planet and her inhabitants. Don't
let egoic concerns hold you back from starting your own chAMber.

Whether you are in a small group or a larger conference,
whether you are a main facilitator or a general participant,
a 5th dimensional being *has access to* .....
choosing certain vibrational qualities,
unthreatened in the expired imprint of 3D.

When We show up as genuine 5D Soul-aware beings, the world is
affected vibrationally and Our Presence is registered.
When We show up as 5D together in a group,
Our vibration is exponentially affecting the world.

◎**Thinking & Action**   ♡**Vibration & Presence**

FORMING YOUR CHAMBER:

◎♡ Make the commitment to evolve in vibrational community with others. This is guaranteed to stretch you.

◎♡ Make friends with your choice of receiving no monetary compensation. Just be in the natural flow of evolution. Breathe in the new frequencies of Self-responsibility and love.

◎♡ Set an intention and allow like-frequencied people to be attracted to you and you to them. Be a galactic pioneer. Trust the Process.

◎ Choose to have a host partner, or not. Either way is fine but help is nice.

◎ Establish place, meeting time (duration 2 hours minimum), and frequency of meeting occurrence. For ongoing community, weekly/same day/same time is easiest and most efficient. *(For away team ground crew, meetings of at least 3 contactees will occur on occasion for a "season" to then replicate. Find a meeting time that works, don't stress.)*

◎♡ Have no formal membership other than contact info for informing on meetings and relevant communiqués. Invite by word of mouth only, without "marketing" or using social media or a website. Include anyone genuinely desiring to attend. It takes only 3. *(For away team ground crew, attract/invite specifically 5D recognizable people, keeping communication as personal and discreet as possible.)*

71

**PRACTICAL STEPS FOR
INITIATING A CHAMBER OF CONSCIOUSNESS**
– 3 –

◎**Thinking & Action**   ♡**Vibration & Presence**

PREPARING FOR YOUR CHAMBER:

◎ Email/text/etc. a blind copy reminder the day of the meeting, with time and address, directions, and maybe some inspiration.

◎ Provide good drinking water, maybe hot tea, let people bring light snacks to share. Eating together is a good thing!

◎ Provide seating (or have people bring their own) and a space that is at least relatively clean and clutter-free.

◎♡ Consecrate the meeting area before arrivals. You'll be glad you did.

FORMATTING AND FACILITATING YOUR CHAMBER:

◎ Casually socialize at first during arrivals and getting refreshments.

◎ Gather in a scircle where everyone can see one another's eyes.

◎♡ Begin with someone opening the chAMber vortex with a vibrational attunement/short opening meditation for emphasizing multi-dimensionality with Allowance and Balance, interconnection with other chAMbers, setting the tone for an experiential context emphasized over the conceptual.

◎ If there are first time visitors, have everyone *briefly* introduce themSelves by possibly having a conversation starter question (or not).

**PRACTICAL STEPS FOR
INITIATING A CHAMBER OF CONSCIOUSNESS
– 4 –**

◎**Thinking & Action**   ♡**Vibration & Presence**

◎♡Establish gentle Guidelines together, based on the 4 Universal Laws of Attraction, Intention, Allowance, Balance, the only real guidelines needed. "Rules" are old paradigm.

◎♡Offer light facilitation and encourage All who are present to be responsible as 5D facilitators to Self-regulate. This can/will be challenging(!)

◎♡Create together conversationally in like-frequency, ushering-in and grounding 5D reality, from the heart. Practice non-judgement, staying true to the intention. This is the fast track for evolving. And please, keep a sense of humor.

◎♡Have an expanded meditation, raising the vibration for the planet, transmuting specific situations and concerns, both personal and at large, for creating the next paradigm. Works well as the closing.

◎ Before dispersing, ask if everyone is "complete" with their experience.

◎ People arrive/depart as they need. Help straighten.

◎♡Know that your chAMber is making a true vibrational contribution in Our world, as a New Paradigm assemblage point of planetary (and galactic) community. Hold the current.

These assemblage points are the foundation for the Self-goverance that is experienced within a new plane of awareness: Freedom.

*For support and further info for holding the current,
do not hesitate to contact Leah LaChapelle; FearOrLove.com.*

CHAPTER 14
*Leaderless, Not Rudderless**

In order to get past the old hierarchical system,
every chAMber 5D participant is in essence,
THE leader and THE facilitator.
Each participant is responsible for
how they experience themSelves,
as uniquely stylized servant-leaders in the group.

After millennia of hierarchical colonial rule of Our planet, where a baseline of victimhood, co-dependence and dysfunction has been instituted on every level, Humans must now learn the way of true Self-determination, both individually and as a planetary community. Living sovereignly within a planetary society, where all beings' essential standing and status are equal, is Our natural state of being! This is the next evolutionary progression for Our species, and Cs of C are a marvelous space for reaching and stretching into that frontier as Self-responsible creators.

Each participant in a 5D group is the de facto leader, as opposed to depending on one or a few strong leaders. **The rudder for this experience is the shared intention of raising the vibration for the planet and creating the New Paradigm, according to what is the highest and best good of All.** The planetary community of the New Paradigm is to be Self-governed. Rather than focusing on that as a reactionary *im*possibility, *try on* Self-responsibility. *Try on* Self-regulation, in Allowance and Balance – regardless of what anyone else might be doing or saying!

In a C of C, facilitating the group's 5D experience and maturation is everyone's responsibility. Here are some essential elements of a 5D group meeting:

*Flow/Energy
*Self-Responsibility/Self-Regulation
*Allowance/Non-judgement
*Balance/Inter-dependence
*Co-operation/Co-creation
*Experiential Context/Now Presence
*Honesty/Integrity
*Consideration/Respect
*Expansion/Pioneering
*Freedom/Security
*Discernment/Transcendence
*Clarity/Relevance
*Lighthearted Fun/Humor
*Authenticity/Intimacy
*Focus/Feeling Complete at the close
*Vibrational/Multi-dimensional Frequency
*Galactic Context/Inclusive of Upper Dimensionals

It is believed that the legendary King Arthur of the 5th century, was to have sat with his knights at a circular table so nobody was ever in a position of power or importance over the other. There is a place for key leadership, and it is within the team, not over it.

A gathering of Soul beings pilots itSelf.

Even a very good-hearted, well-intentioned, and loving leader can inadvertently suppress the growth of the beings in a group, by over-steering, in the name of being "loving", "protective", "efficient", "practical" or even "effective". This can end up short circuiting the imperative of Self-regulating the group's *inter-dependence*. If there is a main facilitator role, a light-touch facilitation is all that is required in a C of C, like the balancing pinky finger is to the hand, as opposed to a dominant leader's thumb or getting their legalistic and corrective "middle finger".

Song "We Are The Leaders"
to the tune of *"Circle Within a Circle"*:
We are the lea-ders,
<Of a> leader-less scir-cle.
There's not one lea-der,
We're All the lea-ders!

As the tyranny of the old world order hierarchy erodes and dissipates, status-greedy, controlling leaders will be considered undesirable dance partners, on any level. It's time for 3D Humans to grow up. Hierarchical, egoic leading and ranking in a group, gets in the way of Self-discovery and Self-responsibility, which are the means to planetary 5D Self-governance.

Says the 5D Self: There is no more caste system!!
I'm "cast"ing off the weight of the ancient ***"caste"*** system!!
*No more "casti*gating" the victimizers,
nor *"cast"ing* dispersions on the victims.
I'm *"cast"ing* my line in the deep waters of Self-love,
and *"cast"ing* the mold for a fully informed populace,
where love and respect for All, is "broad*cast"*.
The violence that puts the "out*casts"* in a *"cast"*, is over.
No longer *"cast*aways", We're All *"cast"* as the lead, in this play.
Let's go to the 5D *"cast* and crew" party!
The spell that was *"cast"* over all the Earth is broken,
and now my Soul's golden shade can finally be *"cast"*.
Now that We outgrew the shadow *"cast"* by the ***"caste"*** system,
Let Us *"cast"* every fear aside!

With little or no orchestration, every meeting experience is naturally unique and is created in the present moment, with whomever is "there" in group-Soul consciousness, for whatever purpose presents. In over 15 years (at the time of this writing), I have never experienced 2 chAMber gatherings that were the same.

*"Leaderless, not rudderless" phrase coined by Paul Norris

ChAMbers of Consciousness
OPENING AN EXPERIENTIAL MEETING

The beginning of a C of C is extremely important. After the natural socializing that occurs during arrival and settling in, it is vital to set the distinctive tone and focus for the gathering, as an established 5th dimensional shared frequency.

**Toning or some sort of frequency attunement
that invokes Oneness
and sets the vibrational and experiential context
is strongly encouraged.**

It is imperative that the context of the gathering be kept experiential. The reason that discussion groups are so common is that many people are more comfortable with the conceptual, mental, or intellectual as the default. Establishing and maintaining a gathering as a multi-dimensional field of experience, will require intentionality to open a vibrationally felt domain. In addition to the attunement, it is very helpful for the host to have set the intentional and vibrational parameters in the space, beforehand.

Attunement through toning by "OM"-ing, "HU"-ing, Tibetan bells, crystal bowl, chimes, tuning forks, gong, etc. are all good ways to set the tone and focus with those gathered, for the highest and best good of ALL. At some future point in Our Human advancement, incorporating this kind of a step for attunement could become archaic, but as of the time of this writing, it is still important.

*The attunement is for a ChAMbering group to
set the intention for.....
assisting in the raising of the vibration for the entire planet.
By establishing a coalesced Presence
which has a 5D energy signature,*
these energy nodes can connect all over the world,
as they attune to the hertz of 5D bandwidth.

No chAMber of consciousness experience is ever a waste, no matter how inadequate it might feel relatively speaking, in answer to what is needed as the full-out planetary-level solution. Though it might seem insufficient, chAMbering with fellow conscious and aware beings is always an honor and a significant investment for Our world.

Even meetings that could have a certain amount of upset amongst the participants, are opportunities for practicing Self-empowerment, and gaining more perspective as the new Human archetype. The chAMbering experience is one in which each individual, and the group as an entity, can be Self-expressed and fluid. ChAMbers of consciousness are for practicing Self-responsibility, consideration, and being teachable as 5D initiates, in a sustainable New Paradigm undergirded by Self-governed planetary community.

There is great joy in being engaged at this level to transform into planetary community. After being reinvigorated in a 5D gathering, participants can each then seed this recognizable energy signature out in the world through powerful personal and interactive encounters. Shake – Open – Pour – En-joy !

In order to maintain the 5D quality and experiential context within a C of C, Self-regulating must be prioritized. Even though this topic has been covered in a previous chapter, because it is so integral to co-creating a New Paradigm, an additional chapter is devoted to further refinement of the fine art of Self-regulating.

CHAPTER 15
Self-Regulating as a Fine ART

There are neither bleacher seats - nor podiums - in this C of C interactive experience amongst unique 5th dimensionals. If this point goes unchecked, however, a chAMber could easily be relegated to a showcase for presenters, debaters, gurus, intellectuals, retailers, business networkers, or opportunists in general, looking for a readymade audience or client/customer base. Even if the subject matter offered by singular speakers is fascinating, the purpose of chAMbering is not first and foremost to receive information as in a formal workshop, lecture, channeling, or Q & A. It is first and foremost for combining with others energetically, in a *co-created conversation.* The conversational voices are to interactively combine as a lush symphony, welcoming occasional lilting cadenzas by the various contributors, that do not monopolize, but do quicken the energetics of the overall shared experience.

Who's Doing All The Talking? When just 1 or very few voices are contributing disproportionately to the conversation, most of the time the imbalance is not occurring because of a direct intention to monopolize. For one thing, in this density, it is simply not within many or most people's skill set to say a whole lot in a few words. Bright people have a lot to share! Sometimes in their excitement, they don't realize that they do not always need to contribute verbally or at length. This is true particularly when they have an extensive knowledge base on the subject at hand. In that case, if the level of interest is very high, it's possible for the group to invite them to speak longer and more comprehensively, but not as a matter of course. An adjunct meeting is always an option.

A C of C is a creative CONVERSATION. Who's Doing the Conversational Steering? In a C of C where everyone is responsible for the overall health of the group, it is up to those in the group to keep the energetic flow going by each…..proactively modeling Self-regulating and contributing constructive content, within the Conversation.

Breaking out of the old mold might seem hard or even impossible at first, but just try it! Participants who may be as yet unseasoned in the fine art of 5D Self-regulating and responsible inter-dependence, can open up a great opportunity for others who are interested in developing this skill further for themSelves and others. When appropriate, participants can kindly help certain ones make the realization that they are actually dominating the conversation, when perhaps they didn't even know it….. *and that it's perfectly OK, and their contribution is appreciated, and let's move on now and hear from others.*

By gently and politely interrupting a verbose speaker, or what compacts into a narrowed dyad, you can bring the gift of facilitative refreshment by interjecting something minty springtime fresh like, *"Hey, you know what? I'm noticing that Marcus and Tom seem to be doing all the talking, and I'd like to hear from some of the rest of Us. Judy or Sam, do you have anything to offer on this?"* Decentralizing facilitation from a single administrator, is simply part of being in the natural flow of a 5D group conversation. Creating a vibrational clearing, where the softness of Allowance can merge with the assertive realignment of Balance, so that a new possibility can arise, is definitely a 5D ability.

It is up to the group to Self-regulate the group!
This is done so elegantly, in each moment,
by *staying present*,
within the *felt frequency* and the group's 5D intentionality.

Formerly, in the 3D paradigm when someone's group behavior was frustrating or "unwieldy", there were several general applications for bringing order. Here are 3 which should be familiar to the reader. (1.) Angry "us vs them", unproductive conflict would break out in the group, possibly resulting in schisms. (2.) The strong capable leader would "handle" the situation and rescue the group, with the group breathing a sigh of relief that they didn't have to bring the balance. (3.) All participants would suffer the effects in silence and "politely" endure the undesirable behavior. Then after the meeting, the head of the proceedings, in their recognized strong capable leader authority, would pull "the transgressor" aside or contact them later to "correct" their loquaciousness, inappropriate behavior, or whatever infraction had been committed.

More on the third approach – guaranteed to stretch you! Even though outside correction for regulating the group seems like noble and compassionate leadership for the group's protection and well-being, it is not distinctively 5D. A leader who brings correction outside of the group, of course does so in the name of reestablishing a manageable balance and maintaining the quality of experience for the whole group. This type of action however, even if it is done sensitively, is generally embarrassing for the correctee, who invariably takes it personally as criticism and possibly as wounding, becoming hurt, indignant, or even adversarial.

Many times, outside corrective measures result in the addressee's ultimate departure from the group in upset and self-justification, finding it all too easy to defame the entire group to others. In summary, "Our strong leader will handle it for Us" approach can breed 3D bitterness and division. Very importantly, this approach inadvertently disempowers everyone in the group, by pre-empting the opportunity to enlarge their capacity for Self-responsibility.

In the next paradigm, consciousness has shifted. Wisdom is Present, much as Human/Betazoid Counselor-Commander Deanna Troi onboard the starship USS Enterprise. (fictional TV series *Star Trek, Next Generation*) Until then, PRACTICE! Self-responsible, Self-regulating Freedom is expansive, not dependent on pyramidal, centralized, or hierarchical structure. **Cs of C are the seedbed for the New 5D governance. 5D rebalancing MUST be done respectfully, IN the moment, IN the group, and BY the group.**

CHAPTER 16
Bringing 5D Balance
and Rebalance

Hopefully it wouldn't happen frequently, but should the vibration in the group conversation begin to wane or plummet, it is up to each participant to discern and feel if this is, in fact, occurring. The best way to facilitate a refreshment of the energy is to be responsible for gauging the energetic temperature of the group. For instance, if a particular conversation is in an unproductive stall, or is veering into counterproductive negativity, division, or judgementalism, first check in with your own Self so that your vibration is as heart-centered as possible. Then simply interrupt the proceedings *politely and firmly* by saying *"Excuse me,,,,, If I may interrupt,,,,, I'm feeling that it'd be good to check in with the group right now. How are We doing energetically?"* And then the group can give input for steering accordingly. This kind of facilitating can be offered from anyone in the group with a true desire to keep the 5D creative flow moving, so that the group's vibrational frequency is offered on a planetary level, effectively.

This is in no way to be confused with bossiness or avoiding subjects simply because they are controversial, (no topic is off limits). Graciously interrupting another participant or a line of conversation for the purpose of redirecting, upgrading, or refining is the means by which a group conversation can regulate, as a group. This needs to be motivated by the highest, best, good of All, and not merely because you might be personally bored or annoyed – there's a difference.

Many times, other participants are incredibly relieved that someone stepped up to look out for the well-being of the group energy, which includes *them*. For so long, Humans have been dependent/codependent on strong leaders and on disempowering, programmed, systems of governance. We simply have NOT been trained in Self-regulating or to Self-selectively facilitate. Cs of C are where We become adept at flowing as a group-Soul entity. All are encouraged to take responsibility for their own experience. The "segues" below are suggestions for steering and dancing with the conversational energy, so that no one is squelched or censored. At the same time, all are to be respected, All are included, and creativity is to be nurtured.

The 5D "group leadership rudder" operates effortlessly in the atmosphere of authenticity. In helping (not forcing) others to Self-regulate, you are Self-regulating for your own personal quality of experience! Consider using the following course correcting phrases for *"crispening". (word contextualized by Jane Chenevert)

Hopefully these *Crispening Phrases will give you some pointers!

*"Actually, it feels to me like We've covered this subject pretty well. I'll just ask, do We want to stay on this topic or is there any other topic that We'd like to discuss this evening?"
*"Excuse me,,,,, I was hoping to hear from some of the others that We haven't heard from yet. How about you, Kathy? What do you think?"
*"Wow Dave, it's amazing how much you know on this topic. I'm sensing that some other people have things to share, so We're going to move on now, but thanks for sharing all of that!
*"I can tell that the <2 or 3> of you are really interested in discussing this..... maybe you could continue your conversation after the meeting."
*"I appreciate your concern about this really important cause. There are actually some other topics We were hoping to discuss this evening. Is it ok with the group if We table this for now?"
*If I may interrupt, I'm thinking it'd be good to get back to having a creative conversation where everyone is sharing. If you could wrap up your comments, We'd like to hear you go ahead and make your point."

*"OK, and let's All remember that here, not everyone is in agreement on every topic, and We like it that way. We like co-creating within diversity."

*"Let's remember that everyone gets to have their perspective without being made wrong. This is a safe space."

*"Everybody just take in a big breath,,,,, and let it out,,,,,!"

*"You know, I've noticed that X and Y are always the ones who bring the meditation/balance/etc. Maybe some of the rest of Us could be more involved in facilitating, what do you think?"

*"If I can jump in here, I'm actually feeling complete with this discussion. How about the rest of Us?"

*"Is anyone else feeling a heaviness as We're hearing these details? I know it's your first time here, Jim, and it sounds like you're in a really rough time. This is a good place for you to be, to see from the highest perspective We possibly can. Thank you for sharing some of what your experience has been. Let's all make sure We remember Jim's situation in Our closing meditation!"

*"You know, this approach isn't something I can spiritually align with, but I hear your commitment. I'd be interested to hear someone else's discernment on this."

*"Thank you so much for expressing your thoughts and feelings. We're going to move on now, but maybe you'd like to host a dedicated meeting for this important concern. Let Us know if/when you set that up!" (Application for Chapter 17 "Agendas")

* --And humor is oftentimes the very best bridge—use it— and use it wisely as the great aligner that it is.

Exercising this level of responsibility to facilitate balance and clarity in a group, is taking some first small steps as a new Human archetype - one who is able to *Stand Forth* in 5D sanity and balance, out in a world having various layers of madness. It's part of the formation of real community. What happens if/when there's "drama" or an electrical charge that develops? In this case, you may find the next chapter which focuses on challenges within a group's dynamics, to be of great help. Realize that hurdles are inevitable! Stay in your resolve to be the Soul-ution, as a group.

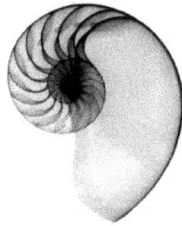

PART 5
EVOLUTIONARY
JUICE

22 ChAMbering 3D Hurdles…..

…..and Their 5D Vibrational Upgrades - WHERE THE EVOLUTIONARY JUICE IS!

Self-governing planetary community does not just magically pop into place out of the habituated, acculturated, well-rehearsed, mental conditioning of the 3rd dimension, by easily and neatly wafting into the new experience of the 5th dimension. Just because people have acquired a little knowledge about 5D, or even great amounts of the stuff, and "say" they want Freedom, that alone doesn't mean they necessarily have the vibrational qualities to manifest Freedom or the maturity to handle it. For first-half-21st century-Humans, the 5th dimension, to a very large degree, is unfamiliar and virgin frontier. A chAMber is a safe place to experiment with conscious awareness for making adjustments to Our dimensional learning curve.

For a group of independent people who each have their own various beliefs and perspectives, it can be QUITE a process to learn the art of chAMbering. **There isn't any one of Us who will do this perfectly on Our own, but together, the enthralling fire dance of "separate becoming One" is executed magnificently.** That's the design!

Here is a list of 22 chAMbering 3D hurdles and
their 5D vibrational upgrades
that for me personally,
have made for fascinating observations
and invaluable Self-discovery along the way:

3D→ FAMILIAR PATTERN HURDLE (pitfall)
5D→ POTENTIAL FOR UPGRADE
(1.)
3D→ Not giving full attention to the one speaking. Having side conversations, which is disrespectful to the one who is speaking, and to the group as a whole; Not being "present"; Being distracting from the supportive atmosphere.

5D→ Be respectful to the one speaking regardless of your level of agreement, by giving them your full attention and by listening. *Having the ability to listen, is an important 5th dimensional quality.*

(2.)
3D→ Being either A.) overly serious with no humor interspersed – or – B.) too jocular and thereby trivializing the mission.

5D→ Laughter is the great aligner. Although the stakes are high and the mission is a sobering one, have a higher perspective and lighten up. *Having an appropriate sense of humor is a monumental 5th dimensional quality.*

(3.)
3D→ Having Guidelines that are not cultivated by the group, with one or a few instituting the "rules and regulations" which results in dogma and rigidity that replace Self-responsibility; Having Guidelines that do not engender the 4 Universal Laws; Not communicating the Guidelines clearly.

5D→ The group creates and establishes the Guidelines and the Guidelines are also upheld by the group. *The 4 Universal Laws are the baseline, and only guidelines that are absolutely necessary.*

(4.)
3D→ Practicing dead ritual and a predictable routine resulting in boredom, lack of New Paradigm distinctiveness, and no sense of magic.

5D→ Shake things up occasionally. Dispense with the typical ritual. Invite different characterization into the formatting occasionally like maybe start from the ending. *Magic and delightful creativity is a 5D quality.*

3D→ Expressing superiority, elitism, exclusivity; Hierarchy; Imbalanced masculine or feminine orientation; Alpha jockeying; Strong personalities dominating.

5D→ Pull in energy for a New Paradigm, relinquishing control, for the highest, best good of All. *Opening to Allowance for all to weave within the shared experience is a 5ᵗʰ dimensional quality.*

(6.)
3D→ Having no outward flow for giving in service – or – Over-emphasizing practical works outside the gathering, consigning the group to be more or less one more focus group.

5D→ Open hearts give outwardly. When there is a need, do what you can to fill it and keep the overall mission focus. *Demonstrable service to others is a 5ᵗʰ dimensional quality.*

(7.)
3D→ Singling out for bringing correction outside of the gathering for a perceived infraction; Not trusting the group to have capacity to bring balance in the present moment;

5D→ Bring whatever the discomfort is, out in the open. Let Love be the morphogenetic field. Correction outside the group brings shame and division, within the group, builds trust. *Non-judgement, discernment, and authenticity are 5D qualities.*

(8.)
3D→ Giving no opportunity for honest feedback or for clearing from previous meetings; Inauthenticity; Enabling "elephants to park in the living room"; No opportunity given for input on decisions affecting the group.

5D→ Get everything out in the open. Trust the Allowance in the room to bring the Balance, without harm. *Being willing to have a loving, recalibrating clearing is a 5ᵗʰ dimensional quality.*

(9.)
3D→ Projecting blame and missing the opportunity for Self-responsibility; Denial of Our own shadow self; Taking things way too personally; Promoting drama; Inability to collaboratively co-create.

5D→ Drama can be entertainment "of sorts" for the short run, but cannot be sustained for the long run. Provide for a clearing after the "storm". Everyone is responsible for their own experience. It is optimum that everyone has a joyous experience. *Taking responsibility for how you experience life is a 5th dimensional quality.*

(10.)

3D→ Showcasing and monetizing for individual profit; Diluting the mission with other pursuits and projects.

5D→ ChAMbering is not a business, it's the scaffolding for Human evolution. For God's sake just get beyond the money thing. *Seeing the bigger picture is a 5D quality.*

(11.)

3D→ Imposing on or taking advantage of the benevolence within the group.

5D→ There are many, many needs. Some will be accommodated, some will not. *Following intuitive Guidance is key.*

(12.)

3D→ Overly-depending on one or a few leaders; Following after and giving your power away to a strong/gifted personality.

5D→ The 3rd dimension is filled with strong personalities. The new paradigm alpha leader is of a new vibrational quality – that of compassion, intuition, proactive service, sovereignty, and bold, Self-loving character. *Meekness is the new boldness.*

(13.)

3D→ Heavily orchestrating proceedings which prevent and pre-empt 'Self'-regulating, spontaneity and creativity; Resistance to facilitation being the shared responsibility of All who are present.

5D→ Control is Old Paradigm. *Trusting the Process is a 5th dimensional quality. Trust the Process, no matter what.*

(14.)

3D→ Allowing without Balancing; Balancing without Allowing.

5D→ Allowance without Balance is low Self-esteem, victimhood, and unworthiness; Balance without Allowance is control and superiority. Both are ego-based. *Allowance is good, Balance is good, Allowance WITH Balance is the bedrock of 5D experience.*

(15.)

3D→ Judging and invalidating the 3rd dimension and its various behaviors; Focusing only or mainly on the world's corruption and not the solution – or – Being completely uninformed geo-politically and refusing to look at what IS.

5D→ Getting beyond condemnation and judgement of what is in the 3rd dimension is a beautiful experience. Let go of the old and embrace the new as it indemnifies grace. *Suspend judgement. Non-judgement is a 5D quality and opens a new playing field.*

(16.)

3D→ Prohibiting *any* discord; Promoting conformity; Religiosity; Unresolved personality conflicts ongoing behind the scenes.

5D→ Bring the B.S. out into the light so it can be healed and incorporated. *Break-downs can be good when they are opportunities to cause a break-through.*

(17.)

3D→ Causing peripheral distraction and commotion; Being pulled off track by provocateurs and infiltrators.

5D→ Masqueraders are attracted to these gatherings. That is ok. They will ultimately provide great equilibrium for energetic creating, as long as no harm is allowed. It is crucial to maintain firm boundaries. *Discernment is key. Impeccable discernment.* (Gary Freeborg's consistent reminder)

(18.)

3D→ Leadership being over-protective, which translates as an unsafe place; Chastising an individual for their expression.

5D→ All are allowed to express their version of the truth. Even if not embraced, all views are validated, without exception. *Keep the context as one of co-creating the Soul-ution, and differences will actually support the 5D frequency.*

(19.)

3D→ Shrinking back from the planetary and galactic mission; Lacking mission clarity, intentionality, and commitment; Too small of a context.

5D→ Who wants to be status quo? These groups are galvanizing the New Humanity according to divine plan. *Maintain uniqueness as a 5D entity that is a planetary community assemblage point.*

(20.)

3D→ Not giving enough love, appreciation, respect, acknowledgement.

5D→ Acknowledgement is given to those in the group who show up and participate, (also for bringing snack contributions, helping with dishes, helping put chairs away, car pooling, making long journeys, etc.) *Gratitude is the North Star for 5D vibration.*

(21.)

3D→ Focusing on conveyance of intellectual information over and above a shared experience; Inability to listen; Dismissive of intuition; Insensitivity to the energy flow; – or – Touchy-feely vagueness with no substance.

5D→ Masculine and feminine orientations are consciously harmonized within each participant. Divine masculine will is in service to divine feminine consciousness. 5D *co-operation just got extremely important.*

(22.)

3D→ Not keeping the evolutionary and creative resolve to Trust the Process and to Hold the current.

5D→ How many ways can We say "Love your neighbor as you love your Self"? We might could say, "Loving your Self is imperative, so love yourSelf the very same way you love your neighbor", and "love your neighbor because you ARE your neighbor!" We are basically integrating and refining Our egos, personas, and personalities into the Soul-aware extensions that We are. *We are One.*

.

CHAPTER 17
Agendas
By the Well-Meaning, and Otherwise

ChAMbering, by its very nature, pulls in the most zealous of players. For the most part, ChAMber-ers are not "tame" - - they are "wild".....! They are also deep thinkers, great researchers, and invariably have intense personal passions and even galactic assignments. These are expressed through the lens of their specific and established projects, interests, set of well thought-out beliefs, and/or concerns. Something for a chAMbering group to avoid, is signing on to someone's "good idea" and following one or just a few persons' aspirations and passion for their particular cause. Narrowing a group's focus in either demonstrable support or opposition, to one or a very few select interests, spells "distraction" from the basic purpose of a C of C, which is to focus on planetary wholeness.

There are many worthy projects! If, however, someone seems to be courting your group for enlisting its energetic support, and it resonates as an "agenda" (to syphon energy by design), you can apply the same communication emphasized in Chapter 16, (end of "crispening" list): *"Maybe you'd like to host a dedicated meeting for this important concern. Let Us know if/when you set that up!"* People who are looking for a platform, fan-following or client base will not enjoy inter-dependent cooperation, or the balance that is made a priority by the shared facilitation of the group. Even though everyone is welcome and accepted, a self-promoting recruiter-type most likely would not return, since there are many other greener "group pastures" than a dedicated C of C.

A Word About Visitors..... A first-time visitor in 3D groups of the past, was generally expected to assertively "make their mark" by distinguishing themselves with their first impression. It was their opportunity to wow the others with whatever they were selling or offering. This is not necessarily so for the energetics in a chAMber! In the 5D group experience, it is the visitors that flow in with the vibration of humility and deference, regardless of their notoriety, accomplishment, or skillset, that very well could be a better fit in community, for the long term.

The 5th dimension is a frequency game, and chAMbers are where We fine tune Our frequencies for transcendence of the old one-upmanship razzle-dazzle surface games. So in regard to visitors who come to your chAMber who are obviously looking for a venue for self-promotion, don't worry. If theirs is an egoic orbit, it will decay in the dedicated energy of a C of C. They will either truly modulate their participation to be in service-to-others, or will move on. Visitors are a blessing, in any case.

Cs of C are not for everyone, and it doesn't mean anything when someone does not choose to participate in yours, for whatever the reason.

Individual chAMber participants will all certainly have specific social and political issues and involvements with whatever it is that empowers them on their evolutionary path. For a C of C that *operates as one entity* however, the very best place for involvement in "divide and conquer" 3D issues, is to vibrationally transcend them altogether! This late in the evolutionary game, the 5D strategy will need to be one of a *vibrational frequency*, as opposed to the futility of the old ways of resistance.

The social/political 3D pro or anti action model has been done before, over and over, throughout history, never resulting in lasting planetary peace. (Some German accents pronounce the English word "agenda" as "again-da", which states the point.) For a C of C to align at this level of activism would cloud that first light of a new 5D dawn, that shines as wholeness beyond binarian duality, and that welcomes the varied streams of diversity. There is an entire mountain range of Human dilemmas to rise above, for shining forth that new dawn Light. It is all too easy for a C of C's continuity and energy signature to become side railed or to lose definition, by identification with any one issue or winsome individual's personal passion, vision, or valiant cause.

Although it may be tempting to mount up impassioned group energy to focus on adopting the "right" side of an issue, it is not advised. Identifying with engagement at the level of pro or con, even though it seems like taking a side should or could make a difference, will water down the alignment to "wholeness". If a C of C group were to be eclipsed by a separate issue, even a very virtuous one, it would mean weakening the energetic texture, hubris, and distinctiveness as a chAMber of consciousness.

This is not to say that there aren't worthy endeavors and stances, because there most definitely are! Embodying 5D as an assemblage point C of C in public view, however, requires that the essential and distinguishing focus be on Oneness. as applied to every issue, not the "right side" of an issue. This is the "non-polarized light" experience. *There will be more said on this kind of extraordinary field work in a later Chapter.*

Operating effectually on behalf of Humanity through healthy cooperation, as an altogether *new vibrational expression and 5D Presence*, is the mission. Standing for world peace is what Gandhi did very distinctively. World brotherhood is transcendent of those issues that are proliferated by 3D egoic, unscrupulous corporations, governments, and institutions. Vigilance and vibrating accordingly from a higher perspective, is necessary for transforming the last vestiges of the left/right paradigm and the holographic energy grid in its entirety.

This mission is a planetary/galactic one. It is to observe All the various dualistic streams of expression that are flowing within 3D, and contextualizing them and validating them, from a higher consciousness interpretation. Vibrating with multi-faceted 5D reconciliation, a C of C inaugurates a comprehensive course for exploring Self-governed Freedom and integrating the Human Soul.

UNFOLDMENT

Flowers unfold and bloom because it's what they do. It is their natural design that they unfold, not because of someone's "agenda" or "ulterior motive" to coerce them to unfold. The purity of a blossoming "I AM chAMbering Presence" needs to be cared for with great discernment. Should a metaphysical envoy with "a great opportunity for the group", seem to be seeking to draft the energy of the whole of your *group-Soul C of C*, get the bigger picture. Realize that even if the opportunity or noble cause is presented with the highest of ideals, it could serve as a distraction from the work of chAMbering that is an essential component in Our great leap in evolution.

What has been afoot here in the galaxy and on planet Earth, is deliberate interference with natural Human unfoldment in 5D flowering. This is due to a secret "agenda" that serves only black magickian purveyors of the agenda, and not the REVEALING of the divine, in Humanity. This is not only a dark agenda, but a cosmic crime. So take time for your group to "flower" in beauty as it unfolds in:

Soul-illumination.
Claiming and retaining Our Souls,
as the rightful heirs to planet Earth.
Knowing Our divine endowment as eternal Soul beings.
Allowing diversity to be Present as an overall Soul luminescence.
Integrating Light's gradient co-creatively
and respectfully for the highest, best good
of All concerned, while Self-regulating with 5D balance.
Experiencing All that is,
as a uniquely individuated Soul,
on Our journey home to Source.

The dark agenda of all mothers of darkest agendas is approaching.

At the end of this Age it approaches as a Trojan horse: "transhumanism and the Singularity". This is a tyranny that could ultimately mean the end of Humanity through the harvesting of Our Human Soul essence.

~ ~ ~ ~ ~

To all Conscious, Self-empowered ChAMber-ers,

All is well. Keep divinely unfolding.

Practice discernment, and do not get sidetracked from

joyfully grounding 5D

as a new life-form

of Self-governing planetary community.

Hold the current. Stay the course!

Flower of Life, sacred geometry

~ ~ ~ ~ ~

CHAPTER 18
Experimenting in Oneness

Throughout history, there has been only one logical, sensible plan to liberate Humanity from the enslavement of systematized dark control. That plan has been for the Light to rise up righteously to vanquish the insidious Dark. That forceful approach brings Us to where We are today, overall, locked in a 3rd dimensional dualistic right/wrong, good/evil contest, treading water at best. This impasse cannot and will not continue indefinitely, because the endgame of the controllers, the Singularity agenda, the complete subjugation of Humanity to artificial intelligence, is drawing very close, very fast.

In Our long journey through the labyrinth of this fear-based reality, there is some good news.....! We are learning how the darkness in and of itself, is actually very useful and expeditious for Our growth and development as 5th dimensionals. For example, in this physicality, seeds are planted or hidden as it were, in the soil where it is dark, where they can germinate. A seed left out in the light will not grow.

Likewise, Human embryos biologically form in the dark ooze within the womb. In Human biological reproduction, if you spill the seed of the male on the outer hull of the female, just naturally, out in the light so to speak, there is no conception and no new Human life form gets created. All that remains is a sticky fluid on the skin, and perhaps a nice memory, for at least one of them.

On the other hand, when the natural process of procreation is fully experienced, the elements of the dark interior are maximized for coming together under the right circumstances, and the mysterious genesis of Life itself is engaged. At that point, a budding new zygote, a unique individual being, is miraculously formed, in that inner place of divine mystery.

"The darkness", is simply the absence of light. The strategy of the lords of darkness, as in evil, has never changed. Their use of violent force, treachery, obfuscation, cold-hearted calculation, and domination over dealings within Human interplay deliberately promotes polarizing separation. This basic "divide and conquer" strategy is for the purpose of self-serving within a hierarchical pecking order, that is egoically driven and misaligned with Source. This is to their *perceived advantage*.

So how do dark and light ever come together, when the dark always does harm? This evolution of the whole is accomplished not by classic judging, fighting, and/or resisting, but by evolving and transcendently embracing the One whole. Growing the proportion of the population necessary to bring forth transcendent Oneness, requires new awareness and a greater capacity to embrace All subsets of the One. **Embracement of the One is only possible amongst those of the Light. Embracing the One whole does not mean condoning the works of darkness or being subject to it. Far from it! It means being Self-empowered with firm boundaries, and transcending the realm of fear, judgement, and division.**

In a Universe with infinite diversity, it falls to the dark to deliberately cause negativity and imbalance. And so it falls to the light to bring such an energetic counter-balance, that an unprecedented expansion of the heart results. This is how a real shift is being brought into the midst of the world, the dark and the light. This shift occurs on a higher frequency than reactive resistance. By design, those beings who are incarnated here into the assigned dark polarity, by virtue of their divisive control nature, do not have the capacity to close the gap of duality. **The dark polarity is utterly dependent upon the bearers of the light to evolve the whole, of which they themselves are a part.**

In this current plane of awareness, if you keep trying to bypass the complement of the dark, to plant your "awakening seeds" solely by wielding the saber of "polarized light", your seeds of

**world awakening will not grow. Your seeds will only take root
and sprout in the natural 5D design medium of Oneness.**

Fortunately, there is now (and always has been in every
generation) a core of heart-based, Freedom aspirants who are
remembering who they really are, and are bringing forth the will to
come out of the negative emotion of judgement. Unless Humans
realize that it is We OurSelves that are enabling the "divide Us,
conquer Us" agenda, the negatively polarized enslavers will
undoubtedly have the winning advantage at the end of this era.

It's late in the game, but after millennia, We are *finally*
understanding. All along, the divine plan has been that Humans
come out of the left/right, "Us vs Them" game altogether, and
breathe newly into the "One-Us-in-diversity" game. If there is
ever to be One peaceful family and community experienced on a
5D Planet Earth, it is imperative that dark and light come together
in the music of Our Soul. This will mean hearing a captivating
new sound vibration, rhythm, and harmony having a brand new
chord structure, dissonance resolved into glorious consonance.

When you look out over your Human family, encourage yourSelf
to see, not with dualistic eyes as in dark and light opposites, but as
All white, All light, in the light of All this is. This might be what
Jesus meant when he was reported to have said, *"Behold, I say to
you, Lift up your eyes and look at the fields, for they are already
white for harvest."* (John 4:35) Definitely allow for contrast, just
view the world not so much in the context of dark/light separation,
but from a newly discovered higher vantage point – a plane in
which We All rightfully exist in infinite Oneness. With that
revelation, the realities of heaven and 3D Earth collide, there is a
cosmic orgasm, and a new conscious creation is born. We as
creators, can then declare with a distinctive voice out from the
wilderness of the darkness, "Let there be light – all over planet
Earth!"

~ ~ ~ ~ ~

FERTILITY OF DARKNESS

"The tiny seed knew that in order to grow,
it needed to be dropped in dirt,
covered in darkness, and struggle to reach the light."
Sandra Kring

While one might feel justified in claiming superiority over the perpetrators of dark deeds, that attitude, in which there is inherent judgement, only ends up serving to keep the immense pain of dualistic separation alive. "Do not harden your hearts….." (Heb. 3:8) the Bible.

Our graduation into 5th dimensional reality is based upon Our capacity to "aerate the soil of Our hearts" if you will, allowing both the light and the dark humus to be the fertility with which 5D beings "grow". **Seeing with full spectrum vision, and validating the One whole apart from dualistic judgement gives Us the advantage.** Herein lies Our opportunity to expand – beyond the twisted ability of the dark controllers to control Us! The light encompasses the dark in natural evolution, as the dark inadvertently motivates Us to do so, and it's all according to the divine plan.

We now have a choice to see and observe, based on *how We CHOOSE* to see the bigger picture, rather than through the keyhole of others' ruthless behavior.

The dark camp cannot and does not create anything in and of itself, which is why the controllers hijack and counterfeit what gets created by the light. Just think how having this piece of knowledge amplifies your light! Likewise, in this plane of awareness, it's equally helpful to know that the light cannot and does not create anything *apart from* the mysterious, unknowable, depths of Creation itSelf, which includes the fertility of darkness.

Integral to Our evolution as a species, is darkness itself. In Our C of C in Austin, We have a symbol that represents the darker shade resonance of Human, that We call "the dark window". In the background, We display "the dark window" in each of Our gatherings. This symbol is never placed above Us, but evenly with Us at sitting level height. The dark is not ever allowed to bring harm. Firm, authoritative boundaries of Mahatma Divine Love are in place! The symbol of the dark window is an acknowledgement of the full complement of All Human beings that make up the species of which We are All a part, even the predatory ones. It is a reminder to Self-empower more than ever, mind and heart, with compassion, and to create from the highest level that We have access to.

There is no more resisting the fact that dark and light complements are each unequivocally a part of the Oneness. Again, in this plane and stage of awareness, neither complement can evolve apart from the other. By proactively and powerfully standing forth in discernment, and diffusing Our I Am radiance into All subsets of the world, We encompass strife and division, on a new 5D frequency, and Our Presence is REVEALED as the causal agency of peace and wholeness. This information comes in handy if your C of C were ever to be "infiltrated", as discussed in the next chapter.

CHAPTER 19
Infiltration .....or Integration

Humans love a good cloak and dagger story. It turns out, We're starring in one! We're in a drama of natural dualistic tension that exists between light and dark, within Our actual reality! We know how it works: The dark seduces and imprisons the light by its lies and deception. This has been the template from the beginning, the continuation of which at this point, is completely unacceptable! (The bit about the serpent tempting Eve in the Garden of Eden is actually a pretty cool story but that revelation is for another book.)

The plot thickens, as they say, in that We have made some new discoveries about the various other players in Our story. Alien-Human hybrids and off-worlders are among Us. These beings *look* Human, and just like most everyone, operate with varying degrees of light or dark leanings in any given moment. Some of those beings can be drawn to C of C beacons. The dark needs their light, to evolve themselves. This is actually the perfect "amniotic sac" in which the new Human archetype can safely develop. A C of C, with its innate light *and* a subtle dark gradient, provides the practice field for healthy scrimmaging. This is basically practicing with friends, for being the bringers of scalable, authoritative, balance and harmony to the world – apart from judgement and vengeance. What an invaluable opportunity for developing Self-empowerment and responsibility within your own community! This translates to your day-to-day experiences, on a world scale.

Some who are quite comfortable playing their role within these darker shades, masquerade as light, preying upon the unsuspecting, and deliberately infiltrate Our metaphysical forums, online streams, conferences, and small gatherings, for the purpose of adroitly bringing discord, misinformation, imbalance, and usurping energy. Others of them, however, may not yet have realized their lineage. Mistakenly, they suppose that their amassed knowledge base is indicative that they are surely "light workers", when unbeknownst to them, they are unwittingly working more closely with a dark agenda alignment, in service-to-self. Regardless, light workers can now see the dark gradient!..... and can validate..... the full spectrum, in gratitude.

When infiltrators are in the midst of a C of C, they are like moth to flame. When discovered by the light, the point is not for the flame to "burn" them, but to illuminate Oneness, allowing their integration. **In discerning the presence of these beings that are darker rather than lighter, do not fear them or reject them at all. It's an invitation for you to evolve by finding your center.** Simply establish firm Self-love boundaries for yourSelf, and also over your sphere of influence in your community. Honor and allow for this co-creative energetic presence within set boundaries. Take care to be true to your light path, and to not be at the effect of any controlling energy. Be grateful for everyone's willingness to play their role in helping the light to expand and to UP their game.

In a radically inclusive group, All are welcome, (period). Not all will choose to remain in this kind of very powerful vibrational atmosphere where there is acute awareness and discernment, coupled with non-judgement, 5D Allowance and 5D Balance. A true infiltrator-disruptor will not be able to be present in this energy for very long. If they really are saboteurs, they'll be forced to adjust their assignment, possibly resorting to tactical influence remotely, or even better, dropping their mission altogether.

How will you know if they are among you and who they are? Whether one is on the darker or lighter spectrum, may be discerned, (not judged). This is determined NOT according to their buzz words, tradition, certifications, titles, diet, affiliations, profession, wardrobe, musical taste, rituals, practice, ceremonies, social activities, or political action, but by their vibration and fruit of their lives. Are they honorable with All? Or does everything somehow seem to always be about or benefit *only* "them"?

Our capacity to truly love will be evidenced in the way that love serves either Our own self-interest, or serves other Human beings. The latter is service-to-others that goes beyond "do good" projects and causes, for the sake of image. That facade is best exemplified when cold, corporate heartlessness is prompted to "serve", only for keeping up appearances for the sake of the public eye (which translates as egoic self-service). In general, stick-on labels such as "natural", "metaphysical", "New Paradigm", "green", "healer", "peace", "5D", "galactic", etc., and using all the corresponding buzz words, postures, or flattering alliances, no longer fills the bill. **Earth people have entered a vibrational reality on a higher frequency, and We now have the discernment to navigate in it!**

It is an enormous blessing to have 4D dark renegades who want to evolve to 5D, too, sprinkled within your group. Even an "intentional infiltrator/saboteur" here and there on occasion, is good for practice! Infiltrators help the light by giving light workers a reason to learn the value of discernment. Infiltrators also help light workers to stay true to their light mission that can only be accomplished through further opening of the heart to the larger multi-dimensional Soul-Self. *Light workers will be forced to examine their own shadow to evolve, by choosing to establish boundaries, and the vibration with which they appropriate them.*

For the light worker whose assignment it is to usher-in Freedom for All, the alternative to separation is to dance within transformation itself, and to creatively expand the existent Universe. This is where We willingly enter into the alchemical void of Trust, within the universal chrysalis. This is where a unique Soul becomes all things at once while remaining distinguished, so as to emerge as a new Human archetype life form. A C of C is where We develop a new capacity to love, integrating all variations of the light, no longer fearing or judging the energies, but ascending for the highest best good of All, within Oneness. This context carries Us into the 6th, 7th D, and beyond. This is conscious chAMbering at its best.

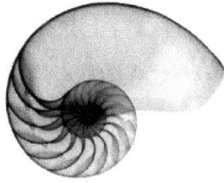

PART 6
AUTHENTICATION

CHAPTER 20
Masculine and Feminine,
Males and Females, Gods and Goddesses

According to the venerable *RA material (Rueckert, Elkins, McCarty)* the most efficient energy in the Universe is Masculine and Feminine energy, in harmony, as complements. When the masculine will and feminine consciousness dance energetically together in a chAMber, it is distinctively 5D. On the other hand, when the masculine and feminine principle are out of balance or have a false balance, just as in any relationship, it can be uncomfortable and ultimately limiting. By "out of balance", this is not referring to the proportion of guys to gals in the group (although it might look that way on the surface) but to the imbalance of each one's masculine and feminine orientation *within the participants themSelves.*

A metaphysical gathering that is influenced predominantly by the masculine will, that edges out or denies the feminine consciousness its pronounced intuitive role, might *appear* to be productive, but in essence be experienced as a controlling, overbearing, uncreative, competitive, and stifling atmosphere. Likewise, if the feminine consciousness is predominant and edges out or denies the masculine its role of reason and action, then the group might *appear* to be spiritual, but the atmosphere can actually be ineffective, unrealistic, vague, irresponsible, and self-righteous. To enable either one of these incongruencies, is the same as putting the greater power of a chAMber, in 5D mothballs.

It is the flow of consciously harmonized masculine and feminine, that will allow a chAMber to enter into the mysterium of a stunning shift in perceptible reality, as an active, cooperative, Christed, creative, Soul-aware, productive, new life form. **When it comes to 5D chAMber participation, the complement of masculine and feminine is vital.** The balance between the two is much more than some reactive pendulum swing away from traditional male dominant patriarchy, merely to only swing back over to the opposite pole of matriarchy, in angry justification. 5D is the bridging of energetic heart-mind coherence.

When *BOTH* genders *are especially open* to developing the creative flow of consciousness *in respect to the feminine principle within each*, it is boldly evolutionary indeed. Opening to this creative complement involves entering into the domain of the heart, to break the mental programming placed in the head. Being willing first and foremost, to tune into guidance through feminine intuition and feeling, can bring balance to the zeal of masculine will, that has classically been prone to aggressively and competitively rush ahead to propound and/or act, offensively.

Using a 3D sports analogy here to make a point, I have heard it said that in boxing, it is effective to lead with your less dominant hand (the more subtle feminine consciousness) and with it, you engage your fellow contestant until such a time as your power hand (externalizing masculine will) comes in to win the exchange, at the optimum time. Otherwise, leading with your power hand makes you a "one-handed fighter", rendering the back hand fairly useless. Such has been the case in Human history in a "one-handed" patriarchal system, with the dynamism of the masculine having been in charge, and the feminine consciousness relegated to a submissive role. That is changing now.

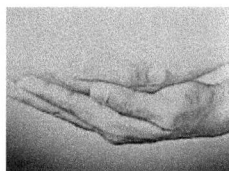 Cs of C provide marvelous opportunities to experience the strengthening of both genders to get in touch with their god and goddess Selves, divine masculine and divine feminine. This is done by co-creating through the magic of the masculine principle in service to, the feminine principle.

The Universe does not manifest in straight lines and angles, but in curvature, which is the phenomenon of feminine expression. Gathering with others in the form of the "scircle" (that's ascension language spelling for circle~spiral~sphere), is a shape that is distinctly feminine. For the purpose of assisting transformation in planetary awakening, this provides a natural protection from the antagonists that operate with an angular/straight line energetic signature. Spiraling energy together in a vortex, with the creative energy of the Universe, is a heuristic, intuitive, feminine energy.

Cs of C are excellent spaces for women and men to develop the feminine energy traits (compassion, creativity, receptivity, unconditional love, etc.) that Humanity needs for superseding the straight lines and angles of the mechanistic power grid.

*With **internally felt** purpose: Trust, know, **BE**, do the Process.*
Being the Process (feminine) is
discovering transcendent power within,
to love yourself free from your own attachments and limitations,
while embracing Our global peace making mission,
so that you experience a vibrational upgrade in your Presence.

*Through **externally expressed** action:*
*Trust, know, be, **DO** the Process.*
Doing the Process (masculine) is
claiming and REVEALING your Soul, the seat of your existence,
when engaging society, and demonstrating
the reality of 5th dimensional Self-responsibility,
as the rightful heirs to this planet Earth.

Very practically, in terms of how to address the subject of gender in your chAMber, honor the heart of the goddess! Make ample room for the passionate women's *feeling voice of wisdom* that recognizes and registers energy patterns. Respect the passionate men in your chAMber! Our men offer *the expressive thought* of god through action, that when called for, alters energy patterns. Humanity is looking for a true oracle which opens the heart portal and amplifies divine wisdom. That possibility is now among Us within Cs of C, and that 5D wisdom can now be outwardly REVEALED and activated, from within.

CHAPTER 21
Being in Action - as Activators

A C of C is not confined to a sit down meeting! To bring experience out of the abstract and onto the practical playing field, it is encouraged that chAMbers *occasionally* have field excursions. It will be a true test to show up as a proactive group-Soul Presence in full view, as 5D non-polarized light, out in the as yet dual world.

A C of C does not gather as a group choosing to be insulated from the outside world. With no conversation topic being off limits, at some point there could possibly be a call to action for some field work. If your chAMber is desiring to be in action out in the public eye, there is a new and empowering way to show up: Not as "activists", but "as Peace Activators"! This powerful comportment REVEALS a 5th dimensional internalized Presence, as an externally expressed interdependent new Human archetype.

I was an activist for a number of years, so I know firsthand that activism is characteristically making demands through polarized resisting, emotional complaining, and in some cases with anger – many times with scant results. Burnout is very high. ChAMbering is not about "activism", in the old paradigm sense of the word.

No amount of traditional activism, with its insisting and petitioning those in the tiers under Our archonic/galactic custodians, will ever restore Our rightful planetary inheritance, or bring liberation for Our species. It will take at least a certain divine portion of Humanity to literally <u>claim</u> Our birthright, not through resistance, but through transcendence of the outmoded polarized system itself.

"Activators" are those chAMber-ers who have grown beyond the existing dualistic right/wrong, left/right structure. They initiate empowering pockets of Peace by showing up as Self-empowered, Soul-aware individuals in their embodiment of 5D Presence.

Activists march <u>FOR</u> Peace. Activators show up <u>AS</u> Peace.

It is admirable that people care enough to voice and demonstrate their pro/anti sentiments. Because activism *does* have its place of relevance for clarifying 3D issues, chAMber-ers will certainly participate in activism on their own, if that is their path of Self-empowerment. However, I must say, making demands on a socio-political control paradigm structure that is systemically incapable of ever allowing lasting peace on a planetary scale, has proven to be futile, and will continue to be. **Activators are no longer content to remain locked in this dualistic discontent!**

When appropriate, the Allowance and Balance that is practiced consistently in a C of C, can spill out into the streets and out in the world. Activators present to Earth their brethren as "First Contact"! **The societal ingredient of visible, coherent, 5D overriding Peace, is what Humanity has been waiting to see.**

A C of C can show up in a cohesive New Paradigm group-Soul vibration to any event, activist or otherwise. You can show up at a location *AS peace…..* and show up *AS 5th dimensional Presence* of whatever it is that you say that you desire for shared life on Our planet. In showing up in proactive Presence, without electrical "charge" or being pro or anti to an *issue*, the New Paradigm is then being activated as the antidote to gridlocked duality. This is the great REVEALING of Self-empowering, Soul-aware beings, having the transcendent 5D Presence of Self-activated DNA.

Your galactic mission is to demonstrate and amplify 5D. This is very different from being overshadowed by 3D issues within which We get absorbed into the high octane of right vs. wrong, which separates fellow Humans. Through the vibrational frequency of Presence alone, your group can proactively serve, by grounding the necessary congruence for transcending the overall illusion on Our planet. "Showing up AS Peace" in a public 5D group Presence, is bringing forth the same vibration that is practiced consistently in your regular chAMber of consciousness meditation meetings. The Presence of Peace is what is proactively modeled by your C of C to the outside world, as the New Human archetype – humbly, yet powerfully and authoritatively, when your group shows up as activators. It is appropriate to give out generic contact info to those who are attracted to this vibration.

➔ Engaging society in direct vibrational experience, demonstrating 5D vibrational reality, is Our galactic assignment both as Soul-aware individuals, and as group-Souls.

Showing up on location as pioneers of a New Paradigm group-Soul Presence, apart from resistance, in the midst of a Human concern/activist event can feel like a trailblazing experience. This is a high level of authentication for a C of C. Until you've had this experience, you may not know how joyous it is to demonstrate just why We are here at this time, as multi-dimensionals on Earth.

~ Stand Forth! ~

Showing up as Soul Presence is a level of Self-realized responsibility that catches on from one person to another through 5D potency, influence, and desire to be a 5D pioneer. No one does this flawlessly; simultaneously everyone does it "perfectly", so there is no pressure! Just relax and let the joy flow, and cultivate Soul connection, recognition, and Presence, in full view.

"Everything changes when you start to emit your own frequency rather than absorbing the frequencies around you, when you start imprinting your intent in the Universe rather than receiving an imprint from existence." Barbara Marciniak

Humanity is still in the time of development for "becoming eligible" to receive critical assistance from the upper dimensional E.T.s. They are patiently and respectfully waiting for Us to step up to become Our higher Selves. Until then, We're going to need some new 5D abilities! Whether engaging in a peace activation as a group-Soul consciousness, or simply living in 5D, it will require new abilities that are discussed in these last two chapters.

CHAPTER 22
5D Abilities and Bi-location

The main purpose of a C of C is for Us to practice 5D together as fully informed Humans, and joyfully grow into a New Paradigm, right here, right now, in the midst of the old paradigm matrix! It's time for letting go of old beliefs and to stretch what We believe, as 5D sons and daughters of liberty, founders of a New Paradigm. One way to reach into the new is to step into new abilities.

As prefaced throughout previous chapters, here is a summary of some distinguishing 5D abilities to PRACTICE in your C of C:
*Application of the 4 Universal Laws (see Chapter 13)
*Interdependent Leadership
*Self-empowerment and Self-regulating
*Vibrational Presence
*Cohesiveness and discernment in place of judgement
*More Discernment, apart from fear
*Alchemy and Co-creating
*Healing, Intuition, Telepathy, Claircognizance, all the clairs, etc.
*Becoming Your Monad and a Multi-dimensional Planetary being
*Interfacing with Higher Dimensional E.T.s
*Harmonizing Masculine/Feminine principles
*Interconnecting with all other ground crews on Earth
*Transcendent Presence that engages the world
*Creating through Conscensus
*Experimenting. . . . . with "Bi-locating". . . . .

. . . . . Bi-location is where the essence of an individual is "situated" in two distinct places at the same time. This is a frequency-based ability that C of C participants are encouraged to experiment with, through the power of Our intention. Being in more than one place at a time is thought of as impossible in 3D. Have fun with this!

There could be those times when someone would like to attend your C of C meeting but may not be able to, yet they'd still like to directly participate and also benefit from the meeting. In this case, they can experiment with placing their energy in two places at once. Intentional bi-locating is a way for Us to move into a lighter density, by connecting with one another beyond the limitations of time and space. We practice by intending powerfully, and tuning into a vibrational frequency where these abilities are possible.

It is of course always appreciated and counted as very positive energy when someone says they won't physically be in attendance at a particular event, and..... that they "will be there in spirit". This is another way of saying even though they won't be there in body, they will hold enthusiastic support for the proceedings in general, from afar. *"Bi-locating" is different from saying you'll be there "in spirit".* Bi-locating is different in that it is specific, highly intentional, and *requires focused action* on the part of both the bi-locator, and those who are physically meeting on-location, to link frequencies.

The following is one idea for how to play with this possibility, but by all means, make it up however you feel is empowering for you. Create stepping stones for experimenting with your energy being at two or more places at once!

How to Experiment with Bi-location:
If you are the one Bi-locating:
1. **Commit** to bi-locate, with the **intention** of being where ever you are physically, AND being energetically in the gathering, at the same time.
2. **Communicate** your commitment prior to the gathering, to another attendee who will announce your intentional etheric presence, at the physical location. If possible, pinpoint where in the room you are choosing to coalesce your energy: Which chair, whereabouts on the couch, floor, next to whom, etc.
3. **Imagine**, and more importantly, feel the group energy

frequency. Lighting a candle can serve as a mooring for Our physical senses, in the knowing that there will be a candle flame in the meeting location as well.

4. **Meditate** for at least 15 minutes anytime during that 24-hour day of the scheduled gathering, in the matched energy and context of the chAMber meeting. After your meditation investment, you may go about your other activities. Note that since the whole point is to transcend time and space, it is not imperative to coincide your meditation with the actual meeting time, unless you choose to.

5. **Know** that you have joined energetic signatures, and that you have docked your etheric presence so to speak, with your group. Know that you are contributing to the quality, texture, and productivity of the meeting, and that you are benefitting as well, in simultaneity, just as though you were there in physicality.

If you are physically On- location in the group:

1. **Announce the bi-locator's commitment** for their communicated intention, and where they have chosen to "be" stationed in the room (the couch, certain chair, on the floor, next to a named individual, etc.)

2. **Light a candle** that serves as an energetic connective point, linking the on-location group with the bi-locator. Groups can also be linked intentionally with other like-frequency groups, by way of intention and declaration. One candle is sufficient for whatever number of bi-locators there might be.

3. **Meditate** in the acknowledgement that there are more present than what is being seen with the eyes.

4. **Realize** that the bi-locator is an active part of the proceedings.

5. **Know** that the group has been blessed by experimenting with refinements of higher dimensions, with both physical and non-physical beings, and bi-locational beings

Happy bi-locating…..!

As abilities go, the art and gift of Conscensus is such a profound group ability, that the entire next chapter will be dedicated to it.

CHAPTER 23
The Art and Gift of Conscensus
[Conscensus spelled with "sc" in Ascension Language]

Saving the best for last, "Conscensus" is the culmination of all that has been shared to this point, and is major 5D authentication. I have experienced this JOY a few times in my community (!!!!!)

"3D Consensus" *as We've Known It* Is…..
…..the *appearance* of general agreement in a group, with varying degrees of surface agreement. The process of arriving at "3D consensus", could include actual agreement, but might entail other elements beneath the surface, such as concession, compromise, buy-off/trade deals, conformity, intimidation, bribery, strong-arming, emotional manipulation, apathy, co-dependence.

"5D Conscensus" Is…..
….. unanimous agreement, reached when a small group chooses to Self-empower in the realm of Freedom, with interdependent cooperation, that results in creating something unique, which wouldn't have been created by any one or two individuals within the group. *5D Conscensus* is arrived upon when the agreement is viscerally FELT amongst All, as a silent, yet resounding "Yes!"

What *Conscensus* Is Not:
-voting (which is concretizing and polarizing); hierarchical (which supports tyranny all the way up the pyramid to unknown levels); majority rule (which excludes and dominates the minority and has proven historically to be vile); representative representation (which is abdicating/surrendering one's responsibility, over to politicians); acquiescence (in the name of being nice and getting along); a task force, algorithm, following a strong leader or leaders, brain logic/mental "mind-alone", strong-arming, endless debate, compromising, co-dependence, or formulaic. These 3D constructs can all be validated in terms of what has served the evolutionary

process, and can now take their place in obsolescence…..!

Conscensus Is a Wondrous 5th Dimensional Art…..
Conscensus is the art of 5D manifestation by way of harmonious and vibrationally unanimous agreement in community. It is accomplished by gathering as One, with at least three participants, each of whom love themSelves in every situation, who choose to enter into the conscious chAMbering creative process inter-dependently. These have a willingness to allow Source energy to combine with their own distinctive energy and imagination. *The result of such intentionality is a view, action, or creation which could not have come from just one or two participants!* It is a process based on healthy cooperation, respect, desire for the best and highest good of all, the power of choice, and trust in the divine nature of the Process itself. The resultant energy is the inner peace, joy, and unprecedented abundance, and creativity of Oneness.

The Language of *Conscensus* Is "Feeling"…..
To consciously align with the seeming paradox of respectfully acknowledging and considering each and every individual's contribution, along with asserting your own choice preference, requires surrendering one's *attachment* to the details of one's own personal agenda. Reaching *Conscensus* includes every voice vibration, and manifests on a level that upgrades to exponential power for all involved. A higher frequency is discovered when an agreed-upon course of action, tangible product, or view as a group, is felt as the well-being of the whole, and expresses through *Conscensus*. *Conscensus* promotes greater Self-love, Self-responsibility, and vibrational Self-empowerment and is literally *felt* by all involved, as an inner and composite "yes".

Conscensing Is Evolving in Planetary Community…..
Conscensus is group alchemy, with every voice registering their choice preferences that catalyze something that did not exist before. *Conscensus* is experiencing the motion and aliveness of

Self-governance in the 5th dimensional consciousness of the New Paradigm. *Conscensing* is choosing to evolve into Self-governing planetary community. In creating a Self-determined future, We take responsibility for Our own vibration in regard to Freedom and learning the value of intuition. *Choosing* the best and highest good of All *vibrationally*, is **an innovative 5D frequency that creates not *in spite of* Our differences, but WITH Our differences!**

How Many Does It Take to Form *Conscensus*?
In order to form *Conscensus* without All those concerned being physically present, would require establishing a quorum. *Conscensus* requires at least 3 participants with open hearts. When learning the Art of *Conscensus*, smaller groups will be easier in the beginning. As people grow in their ability to resonate with one another in their diversity and 5D Oneness, larger groups will also be able to arrive upon *Conscensus*. By starting small and scaling up, with certain post-shift energetics in place, We can eventually grow into the level of 5D evolvement of harmonizing and creating as One planetary people.

Our Choice to *Conscense,* May Be Our Greatest 5D Power…..
All the vibrational voices are necessary to crystallize a *conscensed* choice. We are at this time, learning a greater capacity for: love, power, and wisdom for navigating aliveness in the 5th dimension through transcendence, and with *Conscensus* as a new means to express as a composite consciousness. We are expanding Our capacity to create..... together….. through resonance. Every equal voice is as distinctive as a musical instrument in an orchestra, that when combined, produce a gorgeous symphony, on any theme.

The experience of true *Conscensus* is the crowning, not of the Nobel, but the "Noble One-Bell Peace Prize" for a chAMber of consciousness. Implementing that which is *conscensed* through Our free will, is the next step in Self-governance and joyously stewarding Our Earth, as royal priests in concert with Nature. The ability to reach true *Conscensus,* means 5D authentication.

AND SO THE NEW 5D PARADIGM BEGINS…..

<u>My</u> <u>E</u>mbodiment (of) <u>E</u>arth <u>K</u>inship, or "MEEK", is the new Human archetype status of equality. When standing forth in meekness is remembered and REVEALED by the divine ratio of people of Earth, then the planet and paradigm vibrates and registers as 5D. At that point, **the extreme polarization We've always known, will come to an end.** Even in 5D, there are more (albeit different) challenges yet ahead. On the other side of ascension, more refinements are in queue and await to bring Us toward the 6th dimension of consciousness, and beyond.

There will still be a gradient of the light, with the darkest shades going dormant, at least for a season to later return to provide more "motivation". Dark and light complements will continue to express, *only with more subtlety.* Both light and dark paths will continue to spiral upward as before, in the expanded context of Oneness, intertwining into the *next* era of planetary ascension. The difference between a 3D and 5D-based reality will be a fully informed, Self-empowered, inter-dependent populace. This is sans the pyramid of overarching fear-based control, and incendiary Self-defeating judgementalism. There will be much to celebrate!!!!!

The best We know, We Humans began as galactic hybridized beings, possibly originating from various extra-terrestrial and experimental strains, as a slave race. We are All here in Our diversity, and even though We have differences, when enough of Us have discovered how to love Our own Selves fully, We empower as an entire species. With Our new 5D context, We can exist in symbiotic, galactic, Soul-awareness with the warm-blooded folk, and the cold-blooded alike. We can thrive together in the 5D rebalance, as "mostly vegetarian" lion….. and authoritatively fortified lamb.

Chambers of Consciousness are portals by which to radiate and activate Oneness on behalf of All, in the New Paradigm reality. This reality manifests through the interweaving of spiritually intelligent hearts. As the weavers of deception are invited to meld with their lighter brethrens' evolution….. they can be in healthy realignment with the divine plan. *Parlors of Consciousness*, as we've monikered in this book, will become obsolete. The parasitic nature of their galactic stakeholders will become exposed and disambiguated by the burgeoning sovereignty of Our New Human archetype.

This has been said many different times throughout this book, and since it's counterintuitive to Us, it bears repeating.
REMEMBER:
The dark-role players do not *create* anything on their own.
They can only mimic, counterfeit, subjugate,
manipulate and distort what
the light-role players create from within.
The darker energies give the lighter energies the motivation
to transcend the injurious grip of dark control.
This initiates evolving through Self-knowing, and remembering
Our "standing, status, and capacity" as Human beings.
Therefore, practically speaking,
the light naturally grows and creates, *in concordance with* that
which provides the fertility for growth, namely the darkness.

It is in the transcending of the propensity for judgement and vengeful punishment of the players of previously old paradigm roles, that will distinguish 5D light from 3D light. Love prevails.
~ ~ ~ ~ ~

Cs of C are the basic building blocks for Self-governance now and for Our future society. They allow for development of Self-responsibility and Self-determination, as fully distinguished Humans, within planetary and galactic Oneness. Participation in a C of C, helps to alleviate any underlying subconscious fear one might have for evolving out of the current separation consciousness, and into peaceful cooperation and co-creation. For the highest and best good of All, Cs of C are assemblage points that affect the composite consciousness by **introducing a new precedent for a Self-governed planetary community**. In choosing to form a radically inclusive group relationship, capable of generating intentionally from an intrinsically shared vibrational frequency, the next step in consciousness outwardly manifests. The result is a vibrational frequency for a new Soul standing, status, and capacity.

In a C of C, the inner workings of the group-Soul, by way of frequency, supported by Universal Law, is the governance of the 5D New Paradigm society. Cs of C are the foundational post-Shift framework, starting now. This is only the beginning…..!

Self-governance through ChAMbering is about making room for all the creative hues, tones, and textures that produce exotic new flavors of harmonic blends and pungent scents of relational and co-creative experience. There are no "rules" other than Self-love and respect for All beings. The guidelines of creative I AMness, are provided by the 4 Universal Laws, which serve as the rudder. While honoring One Human family as unique and sovereign, on a foundation of individuated Self-love, and respect for All amidst diversity, personal boundaries are Self-determined. This is how real personal Freedom within a Free society begins.

WE ARE ONE.

ChAMbers of Consciousness
EPILOGUE
When the Shift Fits the Plan

Now We're playing a brand new frequency game. It's the new adventure game of chAMbering, and it's interesting and challenging to ask new questions that beg for higher octave answers! Some new questions: *Who *are* these other people, really, sitting here with me at this energetic communion table? *Do I seem as weird to them as they do to me? *Am I able to have a sense of humor about that? *Now that after many lifetimes, We've exhausted the exploration of Our *differences*, what might We -ALL- have in *common*? *Who am *I*, really? *Can I find mySelf in the whole, *with them,* without losing mySelf? *As I remember *my* own Soul, can I know *their* Souls? *Can I relate with and commune with e group-Soul? *Even though We're each so very different, could it be possible to bear the mark of heart-centered 5th dimensional Homo Luminarians, together?

The chAMbering experiential is like ringing a dinner bell, calling to the children out in the neighborhood who've been very hard at play all afternoon. Innocent children who have been participating in a fantasia of pleasure and also pain, valorous competition with all the accompanying arguments, pretending and playing with toys and make believe, happily and unhappily, wandering and exploring, lost in the serious work of playacting. As youngsters do, We eventually begin to realize that We are actually quite hungry. That's when We hear the familiar sound….. from home. Like a worldwide sonorous mountain alphorn, a galactic shofar is blowing that brings confusion to some and bright clarity to others.

When We hear the unmistakable tone that tethers Us to Our Oneness, We eagerly run home to the sustenance and warmth of family and provision that's waiting for Us. We immediately drop character, give some hasty goodbyes, and head for the sweet threshold of belonging. It's this process of recognizing this transition We're in -- where We experience going from being a grimy little kid pushing, shoving, discovering, insisting, tumbling, crying, laughing, playing hard at I'M King of the Mountain and you're NOT, I'm THIS and you're THAT, to remembering the address of Our heart. "Wash up for supper!" We're reminded. There are manners to be learned and chores to do, and siblings to share with, and We remember that home is good.

Does this sound like some boring adulting reality crashing in upon Us, as the abrupt end of full-out creative play and fun? Is some universal stern school principal killjoy expecting Us to now be mature and well-behaved like stuffy grownups in some higher plane of dogmatic, challengeless, cosmic conformity? Just who is it exactly that is blowing this trumpet blast hearkening Us home?

It is We OurSelves, who are both blowing the trumpet..... and responding to the sound of its call.

True, the days of playing the pretend games of projecting that I'm "The Only, Just Average, Bigger, Smaller, Less, More, Weaker, Stronger, Better, Mediocre, Best, Worst, Higher, Lower, Most or Least" may have passed, but finding out that We're ALL royalty, opens up a whole new universe for reality, in which to create! We found out that it's time to grow up and that there are brand new games awaiting Us. We get to have more fun in endless and joyful Self-expression, as We bring the best parts of 3D: Our true innocence and imaginations, with Us into the 5D!

Who WERE We? A chAMbering group is where We discuss what We choose to create and experience NOW, based on who We WERE and who We ARE NOW.

Who WERE We? Who and what are We right now?

We were the ones behind the mask.....
We were Our father, mother, sibling, Our friend.
We were You...and Me,
dark and light.
(adapted from V for Vendetta, 2005 Wachowski film)

In a chAMber of consciousness, We "wash up for supper", and Our grimy little kid masks come off.   Beneath those masks, everybody looks like family.   The Universe opens up. The dinner bell is ringing and it's time to run home.

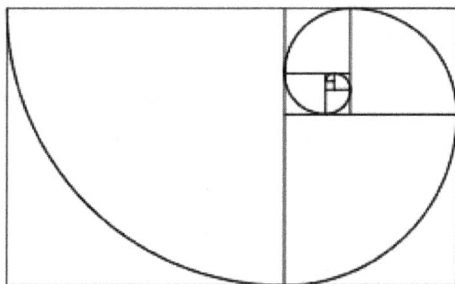

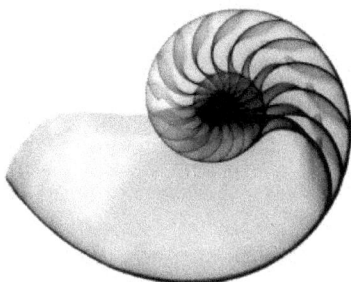

About the author……

Leah LaChapelle is a messenger for the 5th dimension of consciousness, and a trans-dimensional awakening coach. She lives in Austin, Texas with her prime (husband) Wa LaChapelle. Leah has been evolving through scircle dynamics and planetary community, since 2004. Her signature phrases are: "Us luv Us" and "Trust, Know, Be, and Do the Process!"

For further information about
holding the current as the Ground Crew,
and *Waking Up to…..Me!* awakening coaching, contact:
Leah LaChapelle | leah@FearOrLove.com | FearOrLove.com

Other works by this author:

Soul Shade - REVEALING the New Human Archetype (2017)
Fictional novel about becoming 5th dimensionally recognizable.
Companion book to *ChAMbers of Consciousness*
Available on Amazon and Kindle

UNZipping Reality – 11 Steps to Create the World We Want (2007)
Small, good "primer" on awakening, illustrated.
Available at FearOrLove.com